The Marble Statue as Idea

UNC | COLLEGE OF ARTS AND SCIENCES
Germanic and Slavic Languages and Literatures

From 1949 to 2004, UNC Press and the UNC Department of Germanic & Slavic Languages and Literatures published the UNC Studies in the Germanic Languages and Literatures series. Monographs, anthologies, and critical editions in the series covered an array of topics including medieval and modern literature, theater, linguistics, philology, onomastics, and the history of ideas. Through the generous support of the National Endowment for the Humanities and the Andrew W. Mellon Foundation, books in the series have been reissued in new paperback and open access digital editions. For a complete list of books visit www.uncpress.org.

The Marble Statue as Idea
Collected Essays on Adalbert Stifter's
Der Nachsommer

CHRISTINE OERTEL SJÖGREN

UNC Studies in the Germanic Languages and Literatures
Number 72

Copyright © 1972

This work is licensed under a Creative Commons CC BY-NC-ND license.
To view a copy of the license, visit http://creativecommons.org/licenses.

Suggested citation: Sjögren, Christine Oertel. *The Marble Statue as Idea: Collected Essays on Adalbert Stifter's Der Nachsommer*. Chapel Hill: University of North Carolina Press, 1972. DOI: https://doi.org/10.5149/9781469658407_Sjogren

Library of Congress Cataloging-in-Publication Data
Names: Sjögren, Christine Oertel.
Title: The marble statue as idea : Collected essays on Adalbert Stifter's Der Nachsommer / by Christine Oertel Sjögren.
Other titles: University of North Carolina Studies in the Germanic Languages and Literatures ; no. 72.
Description: Chapel Hill : University of North Carolina Press, [1972] Series: University of North Carolina Studies in the Germanic Languages and Literatures. | Includes bibliographical references.
Identifiers: LCCN 72188410 | ISBN 978-1-4696-5839-1 (pbk: alk. paper) | ISBN 978-1-4696-5840-7 (ebook)
Subjects: Stifter, Adalbert, 1805-1868. | Nachsommer.
Classification: LCC PT2525.N35 S5 | DCC 833/ .7

"Affirmation of Formlessness" was originally published in *Modern Language Quarterly*, Vol. 29, pps. 407-414. © 1968, University of Washington. All rights reserved. Republished by permission of the copyright holder and present publisher, Duke University Press. www.dukeupress.edu

The following essays were originally published in *The Journal of English and Germanic Philology*: "The Monstrous Painting in Stifter's Der Nachsommer," Vol. 68, No. 1, 1969; "The Equivocal Light of the *Marmorsaal*," Vol. 69, No. 1, 1970; and "The Human Gestalten and the Fools in Adalbert Stifter's Der Nachsommer," Vol. 70, No. 1, 1971.

"Isolation and Death," (June 1965) and "Mathilde and the Roses," (October 1966) were originally published in *PMLA* and are reprinted here with permission of the present copyright holder, the Modern Language Association.

"The *Cereus Peruvianus* in Stifter's *Nachsommer*" was originally published in *The German Quarterly*, Vol. 40, No. 4, 1967.

FOR PER SJÖGREN

PREFACE

The following essays, written over a period of several years, have been compiled because a number of my colleagues were kind enough to suggest that the essays, being unified in concept, merit unity of presentation. I must confess that the thought of picking up the scattered essays and presenting them in the *Gestalt* of a book appealed to me and seemed appropriate to the general theme underlying them. Therefore they now appear here, in the order in which they were first published, except for the introductory and the concluding essays, which are most recent, and have not been published before.

The concept *Gestalt*, which is used in the essays as the key analytical device for interpreting the novel, was not chosen arbitrarily, but because of my conviction that this concept is central to the author's concern and can therefore best provide access to his fictional world. While the recognition of *Gestalt* in the novel is not new or original with me, the application of the concept to so many of the things in the novel, does add, it is hoped, another dimension to its interpretation.

Since the following studies focus only upon specific details of the novel and do not attempt a presentation of Stifter's *Weltanschauung*, no references are made to biographical data, to exegetical remarks of the author in his letters, or to the variations of motifs in *Der Nachsommer* which are present in Stifter's other works. The present study does not enter into debate about certain matters of traditional interest in Stifter scholarship. For example, there is here neither a panegyric, nor an attack, on "das sanfte Gesetz," there is no speculation about Stifter's exact feelings for Amalie and Fanny, and there is neither a denial of, nor an apology for, Stifter's political conservatism. Moreover, the challenge of labeling Stifter (classical, romantic, *Biedermeier*, symbolist?) and of evaluating the importance of certain literary influences on him (Herder, Goethe, Schiller, Winckelmann, Jean Paul, Eichendorff, Dante, Homer?) has been almost totally ignored.

It was felt that no benefit wonld derive from giving perfunctory treatment to major topics, which have already been dealt with competently and repeatedly by others. The novel, complete and independent in itself, constitutes a whole which is comprehensible without peripheral aids. It can be assumed, moreover, that anyone who has read the novel has also come across general information about Stifter, which is not only readily available, but in some respects more easily accessible than the novel itself with its reputation of detailed long-windedness.

I wish to thank the editors of the journals *Publications of the Modern Language Association of America*, *Modern Language Quarterly*, *Journal of English and Germanic Philology*, and *German Quarterly*, who have kindly granted permission to reprint my articles. They are reproduced here as first published except for some minor technical modifications. All italics used in quotations from the novel are mine.

I gratefully acknowledge the grants given in partial support of this project by Oregon State University through its Graduate Council on Research. I appreciate having had the privilege of conducting a Stifter seminar at the University of Illinois, where the excellent library facilities were available to me.

To my colleagues who have encouraged me — especially Erik Lunding, Eric Blackall, Bernhard Blume, P. M. Mitchell, Walter Kraft, the late Arno Schirokauer, and the late Ernst Feise, I express my warm appreciation. Finally, I express my love and gratitude to my husband Per, the children Jon, Lance, Lisa, Chris, Britta, Rolf, and to my parents Bruno and Elisabeth Oertel for their forbearance.

COS

CONTENTS

I   Introduction: The *Marmorgestalt* and the Concept *Gestalt*   1
II Isolation and Death   10
III Mathilde and the Roses   20
IV The *Cereus Peruvianus*: Illustration of a *Gestalt*   36
V   Affirmation of Formlessness   44
VI The Monstrous Painting   52
VII The Equivocal Light of the *Marmorsaal*: Traces of Mysticism   62
VIII The Human *Gestalten* and the Fools   72
IX Conclusion: Heinrich's Progress toward the *Marmorgestalt* .   88
Notes   97
Selected Bibliography 112

THE MARBLE STATUE AS IDEA

I

INTRODUCTION

THE *MARMORGESTALT* AND THE CONCEPT *GESTALT*

In the center of Stifter's novel *Der Nachsommer* stands the *Marmorgestalt*. Ideologically central to the philosophic structure, the revelation of the marble statue has been placed physically in the middle of the novel, chapter nine. There it is fully described and an account is given of its acquisition and history. In the plot development too, the flawless marble statue from Greek antiquity holds a pivotal position, for this classical, sculpted form is the instrument through which Heinrich Drendorf's aesthetic maturation and his love for Natalie Tarona are made evident. Within this *Bildungsroman*, which deals with the development not only of the protagonist, but of every object in his surroundings, the *Marmorgestalt* is the fixed point.

Perfect, changeless, enduring, the *Marmorgestalt* functions as the axis of the novel. It is casually mentioned by Heinrich very early in the book, during his first visit to the *Rosenhaus* (chapter three). On several later occasions it is also briefly alluded to, but neither the reader nor Heinrich senses its significance prior to the thunderstorm that is depicted in the middle chapter of the book. Heinrich develops gradually and rationally until the moment he is ready to perceive absolute beauty in the perfect form of the *Marmorgestalt*. Then, accompanied by thunder and lightning, the revelation breaks upon Heinrich with the force of a momentous spiritual awakening, and brings his development to a climax. Thereafter the statue is a source of inspiration to him, as he often retreats to its presence for meditation. The *Marmorgestalt* is present in the background of the events that lead to the culmination of the novel, namely Heinrich's marriage to Natalie, the living counterpart of the *Marmorgestalt*. The ceremony, technically solemnized in a church, seems to take place in a deeper sense at the *Rosenhaus*. While the church ceremony is indicated with utmost brevity: "wir traten vor den Altar, und die Trauung ward vollbracht" (VIII, 215),¹ the elaborate description of the bride descending the marble staircase at the *Rosenhaus* poetically recreates the event in its true ritualistic essence: "Dann faßten die Mädchen den Schleier, der wie ein Silbernebel von dem Haupte Nataliens bis zu ihren Füßen reichte, hüllten sie in ihn, und Natalie ging, von ihren Mädchen umringt und von den Frauen geleitet, die Treppe hinunter, auf welcher die Marmorgestalt stand" (VIII, 214). At this depiction of the ceremony the *Marmorgestalt* presides, marking the consummation of Heinrich's striving. In marrying Natalie, Heinrich comes into full and lasting possession of the perfect *Gestalt*. From then on everything in his life has "Einfachheit, Halt und Bedeutung" (VIII, 239). The marriage is the outward sign that Heinrich, having attained complete form in himself, also gains perfect *Gestalt* in the permanent framework of his life.

Philosophical axis and physical center of the plot, the *Marmorgestalt* is also the ideological nucleus from which all the various forms in the novel emanate. As the prototype of *Gestalt per se*, it is the conceptual center of the novel, for it manifests the basic idea: the idea of perfect being projected into plastic form. All the entities within the novel, whether objects of art, nature, or human beings, are modeled after this *Gestalt*, are measured by it, are imbued with its peculiar essence.

The *Marmorgestalt* is the realization of aesthetic principles toward which all things are here oriented. The statue has integrity: it is whole, without blemish, free of all taint of impurity; the material is appropriate to its form; the setting exhibits it to advantage, and there are no distractions either of color or noise in the surroundings; the lighting — direct pure light from the sky outside — relates this art-object to the out-of-doors and to heaven, in accord with its natural and metaphysical significance; the form of the statue is so perfectly fashioned that it gives an effect of vitality; its qualities of "Hoheit, Würde und Ernst" (VII, 130) create a mysterious and magical impression: "jene ernste, tiefe, fremde, zauberartige Wirkung" (VII, 167).

This object of ultimate beauty is a superb example of Greek sculpture, which is the highest beauty in existence: "Das, was die Griechen in der Bildnerei geschaffen haben, ist das Schönste, welches auf der Welt besteht, nichts kann ihm in andern Künsten und in späteren Zeiten an Einfachheit, Größe und Richtigkeit an die Seite gesetzt werden" (VII, 169).

While the grandeur of the *Marmorgestalt* is unparalleled, the other objects described in the novel also to some extent adhere to the aesthetic principles exemplified by the *Marmorgestalt*. All of the configurations within this novel are presented as aesthetic phenomena, and by being perceived as *Gestalten*, they are drawn into the orbit of the perfect *Gestalt*.

Once awakened to beauty, Heinrich becomes aware of many lovely forms around him. He finds, for example, that the grotto nymph is "ein sehr schönes Gebilde" (VII, 130), and he contrasts this statue with the *Marmorgestalt* in terms reminiscent of Schiller's "Anmut und Würde": "Wenn auch jenes an Hoheit, Würde und Ernst weit den Vorzug in meinen Augen hatte, so war dieses doch auch für mich sehr anmuthig, weich und klar" (VII, 130). While not an awe-inspiring presence, the grotto nymph charms Heinrich with loveliness. The luminous white marble of the nymph is enhanced by the backdrop of dark green ivy; the ever-trickling water conveys the mood of serenity; the two majestic oaks "guarding" the nymph on both sides offer contrastive balance to her graceful form.

Everywhere there are objects related to the *Marmorgestalt*. In his parental home Heinrich finds carved gems with the imprint of classical beauty. Their configurations look so inevitable as if nature had determined them ("wie Naturnothwendigkeiten" VII, 169). The spirit of classical antiquity expressed in these ancient cameos can come to life in modern jewelry as well, if the jewels are placed within a proper setting which enhances but does not dominate them (VII, 180), and if the whole piece is organically unified to be "ein zusammen gehöriges, in einander gewachsenes Werk" (VIII, 221). For example, Natalie's emerald pendant, described as heroic ("heldenartig" VIII, 223), gives the same impression of awe, mystery, and exotic beauty as the *Marmorgestalt*: "etwas Ernstes, Feierliches, fremdartig Schönes" (VIII, 223).

The principle that the integrity of every *Gestalt* must be maintained is illustrated most strikingly by Risach's marble collection. Made up entirely of specimens gathered by Risach, it cannot accommodate the marble slab which Heinrich offers Risach as an addition. The new marble slab, unrelated to the already existing pieces, would impair the homogeneity of the collection. Risach graciously accepts the inappropriate gift, but uses it for some other purpose.

Vitality and naturalness are important aspects of all objects. The *Marmorgestalt* looks so much alive that the maiden seems to breathe; the ivy rustling about Drendorf's old weapons and twining up the window of his museum room gives a lifelike quality to the hard objects there. At the *Sternenhof* the entire mansion is exposed to the influence of external nature. The rooms, arranged in a straight line with windows along both sides, offer simultaneously the sight of the art-objects within and the landscape outside. In summer the windows are opened, and air flows into the rooms, uniting the realms of art and nature so that one is "halb im Freien und halb in der Kunst" (VI, 320).

All objects, even formations in external nature, are here drawn into relation with the *Marmorgestalt,* because they are all, potentially at least, *Gestalten* blending nature and art. A garden, such as the Maklodens', for example, is a landscape transformed by art into a unified and pleasing whole ("zu einem sehr schönen Ganzen zusammengestellt" VIII, 115 f.). Risach's entire estate is such a balanced *Gestalt* wherein everything looks as if it had grown together as a unity and nature is presented to best advantage (VI, 135).

Human beings too are *Gestalten* which can be looked upon as art works. So for instance, Natalie in her wedding jewelry is like a priceless object within a "frame" of jewels (VIII, 223). In another scene she is posed among beautiful medieval furnishings within a double frame of two doors, creating a picture which has rightly impressed scholars by its resemblance to an exquisite painting. As an aesthetic image, Natalie projects the idea of fulfillment, as Heinrich notes: "Ich verstand auch, was die Gestalt sprach, ich hörte gleichsam ihre inneren Worte: 'Es ist nun eingetreten!'" (VII, 301). Natalie and the *Marmorgestalt* are both images of fulfillment, which is the ideological goal of every *Gestalt* and one of the basic ideas of *Der Nachsommer*. Serene, complete, perfect within their own beauty, the forms draw Heinrich the protagonist toward his own fulfillment.

Gestalt has to do with orderly structure, balanced form, pleasing configuration. The term may denote an *object* perceived in such categories or it may pertain to the inner or outer *qualities* of such an object. In the first instance an object is a *Gestalt*; in the second, an object has a *Gestalt*.

The perception of *Gestalt* may derive from the perceiver as a subjective phenomenon of psychological origin, or it may derive objectively from the being of the object itself and thus belong to the field of philosophy or metaphysics. Whether it should be thought of as a psychological or a metaphysical phenomenon — or both — need not concern us here, and would post-Kant be impossible to determine. A mind highly oriented to the *Gestalt* concept tends to project the idea of *Gestalt* into everything and to see everything as a manifestation of *Gestalt,* either by projecting his mental concept into the object or by recognizing such a principle inherent in the object. Universally applied, the concept becomes an idea which provides the basis for a philosophy of cosmic order and universal harmony.

The author, describing things, people, abstract notions, landscapes, human relationships — everything, in fact — in terms of form, uses the word *Gestalt* within a wide spectrum of meanings, including the meanings of physical shape and of inner form; but, in general, the author tends to endow the term with merit and to apply it, above all, to beautiful and noble things.[2] Aesthetic and ethical considerations readily attach themselves to the idea of shape and form, for it is a small step from viewing *Gestalten* as they are, to desiring that they be good and beautiful. In this novel with the prime image of the *Marmorgestalt* the teleological thrust of the term is particularly strong.

For Stifter the term also has pronounced religious connotations.

Although already in the eighteenth century the concept is imbued with pantheistic feeling, the term takes on a more distinctly doctrinaire theistic quality with Stifter and reflects the author's early absorption of the Roman Catholic atmosphere at the Kremsmünster monastery school, along with his adoption of the liberal aesthetic views of the German classical period. In a world view where God is the origin of creation, a *Gestalt* in essence is a manifestation of the Deity. In the *Gestalten* of *Der Nachsommer* the Godhead assumes visible concrete forms, and their order and beauty give evidence of His Spirit within.

The common metaphysical basis of all *Gestalten* in *Der Nachsommer* determines that fundamentally all things are alike, in that all things contain the same spiritual substance. Nature, art, and man are thus related, and each object, from whatever realm, is charged with perfecting itself. Man as both *Gestalt* and *Gestalter* is uniquely entrusted with the task of developing his own form and of assisting the objects around him to develop theirs. As creator and keeper of *Gestalten*, man is somewhat akin to the Deity.

The underlying Divinity of all things relates them to each other and establishes a harmonious, interrelated world. *Der Nachsommer* illustrates an orderly cosmic system wherein *Gestalten*, like Leibnizian monads, all move toward highest self-realisation.[3] Unlike monads, however, these *Gestalten* do not surge ever upward, but merely unfold and develop. The philosophic system underlying this novel lacks the dynamism of the Leibnizian scheme where individual centers of force perpetually strive to ascend the scale of being infinitely to the Godhead. The goal of Stifter's *Gestalten* is a static one. Fullness of being, once reached, remains steady in its own radiance. The question whether such perfection is actually possible in the real world is irrelevant. In the fictional world of *Der Nachsommer* perfection is not only attainable; in the *Marmorgestalt*, notably, it is realized.

Der Nachsommer has been called a "hieratic didactic poem"[4] and an "illustrated code of law."[5] The novel is a vehicle the author uses to expound the aesthetic-ethical principles of *Gestalt* as he inherited them from the classical tradition of the eighteenth century and modified them according to his personal background and observations. Every phenomenon is measured here against its ideal form, is silhouetted against the bright sun of the *Gestalt* idea. Back of each object of nature or of art stands the Platonic idea, here endowed with Divinity.

While *Gestalt* is the intended message, this concept does not make up the total reality of *Der Nachsommer*. Less obvious, less edifying, and less comforting, there looms behind the *Gestalt* principle the ominous shadow of *Gestaltlosigkeit*. The passing of time, man's carelessness and egotism, man's passions, and an unfeeling heaven are all recognized as powers inimical to the forms. Risach and his men are engaged in the constant and desperate effort to rescue all the *Gestalten* from the forces threatening dissolution.

Beneath the optimistic view that the world is a system of universal harmony manifesting the Divine, there lowers a dark current of pessimism and foreboding. The author knows that beyond the earth is infinite space, beyond life and form there is death and decay. Surrounding the magnificent edifice of existence erected by this novel there is an abyss of nothingness.

The fog in the low-lands, the blue haze enveloping the autumn landscape, the destructive force of rain upon the configurations of snow — these are some reminders of the basic reality of formlessness. Heinrich's geological surveys show him that the history of the earth is a history of death upon death, while the infinite stars above him blaze out their cosmic indifference to man.

The people in *Der Nachsommer* are aware also of disorder within the ego, that vast landscape of rubble and ruin. Egotistical passions spring from this inner disorder, inevitably bringing about guilt and chaos, as Fritz Martini points out: "Die Schuld führte in das Ungesicherte, das Chaos: es ist nicht seine Strafe, sondern seine immanente Folge."[6] The tension between man's passions and God's law brings about, according to Victor Lange, a power struggle which can be described as "existential."[7] The existential struggle depicted in *Der Nachsommer* is not as circumscribed as Lange perceives it, however. It is not limited to the ethical plane, where man is in disharmony with the divine order. It is rather an existential struggle enacted on the cosmic scale between the elementally opposing forces of form and formlessness, creation and chaos, being and nothing, *Gestalt* and *Gestaltlosigkeit*. Man is not the fundamental cause of the combat, but merely a part of it and a witness to it.[8]

The author, an interested witness, has created in *Der Nachsommer* a bulwark against the threatening *Nihil*. The abundance of the *Gestalten* in the novel have been created to cover up the vast nothing of formless, meaningless space. As Walther Muschg states: "Die schönen Dinge beanspruchen im *Nachsommer* deshalb so viel Raum, weil sie das Chaos verdecken müssen, das hinter ihnen lauert."[9] The novel is both a monument to the *Gestalt* and a memorial of man's war against inevitable annihilation.

As all philosophies, the philosophy expressed and lived by the characters of *Der Nachsommer* is inadequate to our empirical reality. The establishment of an élite society engaged in agrarian management and the restoration of historic art objects seems utopian, and perhaps not particularly desirable; the most pressing problems of our world are not solved by the *Gestalt* ethic; the very notion of perfectability is questionable. Still, scholars, such as Horst Glaser, who pass negative judgment upon *Der Nachsommer* on these grounds,[10] are missing the real significance of the work.

Der Nachsommer commands our attention not for its presentation of empirical reality — each man's empirical reality is, after all, his own. The reality this novel projects has existential dimension. The terror that seems to underly the forced serenity and compulsive orderliness of the *Rosenhaus* suggests a condition more familiar to modern readers than to those of Stifter's day — "Angst vor der Absurdität des Lebens."[11] The novel depicts the most fundamental endeavor of existential man. Heinrich and Risach with their friends are engaged in the enterprise of wresting form from chaos and creating a meaningful order of existence for themselves and for all the entities in their world. The novel may be summed up as "eine einzige große Geste der Aufforderung, 'Wesenheit' zu erschließen."[12] The *Marmorgestalt* is an existential symbol of Being: perfect, fulfilled, eternal.

Perhaps the novel itself should be evaluated according to the principles it sets forth. What matters about any creation is that it have integrity, that its parts relate to the whole, that it present a coherent image, that it invite contemplation and glow with an inner beauty. Where style is appropriate to idea, matter to shape; where the whole is animated by an aesthetic-ethical spirit, there we have a significant *Gestalt* which brings to man a kind of blessing and solace. *Der Nachsommer* is such a work.

II

ISOLATION AND DEATH

The idyllic harmony that suffuses Stifter's novel has been widely discussed and analyzed by scholars in the field,[1] but less attention has been given to the undercurrent of sadness, which, in the words of Walther Rehm, is "hidden between the lines."[2] A new dimension to our understanding of *Der Nachsommer* — described by one writer as "inexhaustible in its mystery"[3] — can indeed be added by further probing into the disturbances that lie beneath the smooth exterior of the novel.[4]

The feeling of isolation experienced by the characters in *Der Nachsommer* presents an element of disquietude well worth exploring. As we trace this motif through its many forms in the novel, light is cast upon otherwise unrevealed emotions experienced by the characters. Observing how they cope with the problem of isolation, we attain a deeper insight into the philosophy underlying the world of *Der Nachsommer*. In extreme isolation the characters are even confronted with the image of death, which emerges as a bold dissonance to challenge the vision of a perfect world that the author intended to make manifest in his work.

Einsamkeit, a concept containing both the positive and negative emotional overtones of solitude, isolation, and lonesomeness, is a feeling and state familiar to all the main characters in the novel. *Einsamkeit* does in fact pervade their lives. Heinrich, as a young boy, is always somewhat ill-at-ease in society and appreciates his home as "eine holde, bedeutungsvolle Einsamkeit" (VI, 217);[5] the ladies at the *Sternenhof* alleviate "unsere Einsamkeit" (VII, 309) by cultivating the arts; Heinrich's father is isolated in his deepest interest until Heinrich grows up (VII, 171); even Roland, the passionate artist, is described by Heinrich as "ebenso vereinsamt unter den Menschen...wie ich" (VII, 228).

For Risach, the sage and mentor, *Einsamkeit* is an ethical imperative. He has withdrawn from the world of urban society, which he regards as corrupt and degenerate, and lives in relative seclusion upon his landed estate. By creating in his *Rosenhaus* the nucleus of an ideal society, he hopes to preserve the cultural values that are threatened in the world outside, and to transmit them to the next generation. The force which Risach in his isolation exerts upon the world is symbolically represented by the powerful attraction which the isolated white *Rosenhaus* exerts upon young Heinrich, who, as a wanderer, finds shelter there from a storm brooding outside. Risach's home "mit einladendem, schimmerndem Weiß (VI, 43) still glows while the rest of the landscape (with the exception of the church steeple)[6] lies "im Schatten" (VI, 43). The light symbolism used here seems to express the author's conviction that the forces of evil brooding over the world cannot overshadow all while there is yet a lonely individual who combats these forces with his whole existence.

Einsamkeit is an important element in both love-stories in the novel. Long before Heinrich and Natalie become acquainted socially, they share a poignant moment, when at a performance of *King Lear* grief overwhelms both and isolates them from the rest of the audience. As their eyes meet, Natalie's sense of aloneness in the crowded theatre, "wo ich sonst vereinsamt gewesen wäre" (VII, 285), is relieved by her communion with someone as sensitive and responsive to an aesthetic experience as she.

Later, the erotic attraction developing between Heinrich and Natalie is never alluded to explicitly until the actual engagement takes place, but it can be intuited,[7] especially from their otherwise unexplainable flights into solitude. To be sure, it is Heinrich's work that takes him into isolated regions, but there he can often be found gazing purposelessly off into the landscape (VII, 123). Later he confesses to Natalie that during these moments of isolation, "wenn ich auf den Höhen der Berge war, ... wenn ich auf die festen, starren Felsen blickte, ... wenn ich auf die Länder der Menschen hinaus schaute" (VII, 284), it was her presence he felt.

For Natalie there is no practical need to take long walks in the heat of the day, as she does, but she declares that they afford her opportunity for reflection and seclusion ("Als Bestes bringt der Gang, daß man allein ist, ganz allein, sich selber hingegeben" VII, 221). In her confession to Heinrich that she felt pain for his sake when she was wandering over the fields ("Ich habe manchen Schmerz um Euch empfunden, wenn ich in den Feldern herum ging" VII, 283), the reader is given a clear indication that her restlessness was brought on by her longing for Heinrich, and that through solitude she sought to regain her composure.

When Stifter's characters seek solitude, they are not merely trying to get away from others, they may be trying to find themselves. Alone, they strip themselves of pretense and illusion and enter into a sacred and private realm. Their soul in this state experiences shock when it is suddenly exposed. Natalie is profoundly startled ("sie erschrak sehr" VII, 208) when she finds Heinrich present upon her return from a walk, and he too is "beinahe erschrocken" (VII, 208) to catch her thus unawares. On another occasion, when the two meet by chance while taking solitary walks, they are again startled ("Wir erschraken Beide" VII, 216). After a conversation about the blessings of aloneness, they do, however, then walk back to the house together. This act signifies that they have come closer to each other in spirit and can now share the realm of solitude.

A real crisis in their relationship occurs when Heinrich blunders in upon Natalie's retreat from the gathering at the *Sternenhof* party. In the grotto she sits alone on a marble bench, resting her forehead upon her hand ("barg die Stirn in ihrer Hand" VII, 241) in a gesture indicating emotional distress. Heinrich, who has likewise sought solitude, finds himself unexpectedly before Natalie and at a complete loss ("Ich blieb stehen und wußte nicht, was ich thun sollte" VII, 241). Not wishing to intrude, he tries to withdraw immediately,[8] but Natalie has seen him, and, disconcerted, she rises and flees ("mit beeilten Schritten" VII, 241). Thereupon Heinrich takes her place on the bench and sits for a long time regarding those objects: the trickling water, the alabaster bowl, the glowing marble, which are vitally present during their later love scene and somehow mystically related to their love. Though he doesn't mention Natalie's name except to point out that this is the bench upon which Natalie has been sitting, there is no doubt that his thoughts are about the girl, whose sudden flight might be interpreted as hostile to Heinrich. Later, during the engagement scene, he admits that her deliberate avoidance of him caused him grief.

The estrangement between them ("mit Natalien war ich...beinahe fremder" VII, 272) is still present a year later, during Heinrich's next visit. Once again Heinrich accidentally surprises Natalie at the grotto. They are both startled, and she rises in confusion, as if to flee again. This time, however, Heinrich does not remain passively silent, and the awkwardness of the previous occasion is not repeated, but is resolved. Heinrich, now more mature and self-assured, establishes himself as master in their relationship. He helps Natalie regain her composure by apologizing for his intrusion. With exquisite tact he invites her to state her wishes: should he leave or stay? Thus guided, Natalie allows her true feelings to express themselves, and the misunderstanding engendered at the previous grotto encounter is cleared away. Their love, prefigured many years before during the performance of *King Lear*, when they briefly shared an aesthetic experience of tragedy, is brought to radiant fulfillment here in the shrine of the marble nymph. Within the realm of art and beauty, isolated from the world, they find communion with each other.

Einsamkeit shows its tragic aspect in the youthful love affair between Risach and Mathilde. In early childhood Risach loses his father. Since his mother is the sole object of his affection during his formative years, Risach experiences a deep depression when she dies, and thereafter leads a lonely life ("ein sehr zurückgezogenes Leben" VIII, 104). When his sister, the last remaining member of his family, also dies, he shuts himself off even further from people and joy ("Ich zog mich nun noch mehr zurück, und mein Leben war sehr trübe" VIII, 105).

He is rescued from despondency by the position he takes with the Makloden family, who employ him as companion to their two children. In this new home he experiences an upsurge of happiness, which is heightened by the tender and passionate relationship that develops between him and Mathilde, the adolescent daughter of the house. When he is asked to renounce her because of her youth and his own unreadiness to assume family obligations, he feels that nothing is left him ("Jetzt bin ich ganz allein. Mein Vater, meine Mutter, meine Schwester sind gestorben" VIII, 147). Loss of her, climaxes the bereament he has already experienced. Expelled from the Maklodens' home, rejected finally also by Mathilde, who fails to understand his acquiescence in her parents' demand, he plunges from the ecstasy of reciprocal love into a state of desolation ("verödet, wie ich früher nie verödet gewesen war" VIII, 158 f.). Day after day he climbs a steep cliff and stares down into the abyss. He recalls that as a child he used to throw rocks down from the ledge. So vividly does Risach describe the rocks as they hurtle down to their destruction that he seems to undergo his own death in the image of "der Geworfene."[9] Suicide is indeed in his mind, and he is saved from its horror ("unklare, schauerliche Vorstellung" VIII, 159) only by the memory of his mother and her love. The isolation motif and the death motif here merge: in its most extreme manifestation isolation takes the form of death.

In view of Risach's contemplated suicide one cannot agree with Walther Rehm that death is not present in the novel.[10] Nor is it correct to say that no one dies in *Der Nachsommer*.[11] On the contrary, the author underlines the fact and the tragedy of death by bringing into the novel the names of numerous people whose only significance rests in their dying. In Risach's account of the past he dwells morbidly on the death, first of his mother, then of his sister. In Drendorf's narration all of the following persons are mentioned but given little or no function, except to die: his old tutor, parents, employer, sister, brother, grandparents, and great-uncle. Drendorf even projects his own and his wife's death upon Heinrich's mind by reminding him to love his sister when the parents are gone ("wenn auch wir allein sein, und er und die Mutter im Kirchhofe schlummern würden" VII, 191). The two older men do not avoid mentioning death, but speak of it calmly, with acceptance and faith. Drendorf expresses his attitude thus: "Man müsse erwarten, was Gott gewähre" (VIII, 12), and Risach: "Es wird hier, wie überall, gut sein: Ergebung, Vertrauen, Warten" (VII, 155).

Heinrich Drendorf also experiences the absolute isolation of death, in an episode whose significance has been heretofore completely overlooked by critics. One summer Heinrich undertakes a geological survey of the mountains, and during this undertaking he has a moment of revelation comparable in significance to the moment when he becomes fully aware of the beauty of the marble muse.[12]

The author introduces the mountain episode with an unexplained feeling of distress in the depths of Heinrich's being ("etwas Unliebes in dem Grunde meines Innern" VII, 195), thereby establishing the mood of this episode and giving us a clue to its meaning. As Heinrich leaves a familiar inn, his feelings are expressed once more ("mit einem wehmüthigen Gefühle" VII, 195), but from then on nature takes over the function of expressing Heinrich's inner state.[13] Close attention to the details of the rich imagery in this episode and a careful scrutiny of Heinrich's surroundings will reveal that the author is concerned here with much more than a physical scientific survey. The episode represents an existential crisis and constitutes a climax in Heinrich's emotional development.

Heinrich finds that the forests he enters are forbidding and ugly ("Weit verzweigt und wild verflochten,...aber nicht schön" VII, 195).[14] The next inn is described as a prison ("Mauern, mit grünem Moose bewachsen, bildeten mein Haus" VII, 196), and the iron crosses at the small windows of the sparsely furnished room even suggest a place of death. Decay is apparent in the adjacent garden, which has fallen into ruin ("ein zerfallenes Gärtchen" VII, 196). *Schnittlauch*, the only plant growing there, is ordinarily raised only to be cut down, and its very name brings to mind the grim reaper ("ein Schnitter, der heißt Tod") of the old folk-song.

The valley is too confining, "eng," and the woods too dark, "finster," to allow for a view of the snow peaks above (VII, 196). Blackness imbues nature. Like a mythical giant the sinister presence of the black forest asserts itself: "Schwarzer Tannenwald sah auf meine Fenster, schritt an den Bächen...und zog sich auf die Berge" (VII, 196). In the depth of night he reads the works of a writer "der schon längst gestorben war" (VII, 200). As he reflects upon that "condition (Zustand) even more unfathomable (unergründlicher) than sleep," the images used by the author, the snuffing of the candle, the closing of the eyes, are death images (VII, 201). The patrons of the inn are *black* teamsters, drawing their *black* load of coal up a *gloomy* road. The deliberate repetition of the word "black" in the following passage; the use of the word *ungeheuer* with its overtones of "monstrous, frightful"; the slow and heavy dactylic tread of the cadence evoke the mood of a funeral procession: "Auf der Gasse war der Boden *schwarz*, und dieselbe *Schwärze* zog sich in das Gras hinein; denn das Einzige, welches häufig an diesem Wirthshause ankam und da hielt...waren Kohlenfuhren. In dem ganzen bei näherer Besichtigung sich als *ungeheuer* zeigenden Waldgebiete waren die Kohlenbrennereien zerstreut, und ganze Züge von den *schwarzen* Fuhrwerken und den *schwarzen* Fuhrmännern zogen die *düstere* Straße hinaus." (VII, 196).

With the death-mood well established, the author shows Heinrich and his men carrying on their geological studies. They explore the woods, they investigate the rock formations and gather samples of all the varieties, they pursue the course of the streams. In the grandeur of the primeval forest they see the enormousness of nature, its indifference to man and its destructive power. The presence of death can be sensed in the dark shadows ("in dem dunkeln Schatten") of the woods and in the dead tree-stumps ("erstorbene Stämme" VII, 198). Beyond the timber line the world of rock, devoid of plant life, appears even vaster than the forests. Heinrich penetrates regions so remote and harsh and desolate that he can describe them only in superlatives: "In die wildesten und abgelegensten Gründe führte uns so unser Plan, auf die schroffsten Grate kamen wir" (VII, 198). In this awesome and terrifying mountain region menacing images emerge before Heinrich: a vulture, a fluttering thing of no identity, a wooden arm jutting out into the isolation ("wo ein scheuer Geier oder irgend ein unbekanntes Ding vor uns aufflog und ein einsamer

Holzarm hervor wuchs, den in Jahrhunderten kein menschliches Auge gesehen hatte" VII, 198 f.). The higher Heinrich ascends, the more he becomes aware of the tremendous power of a nature inimical to man.

The response that Heinrich and his men make to the challenge of this arch-enemy is one of defiance. They literally strike out against nature, as with hammer and chisel they cut into the smooth rock walls to break deep holes into them and drive in their iron spikes ("wenn wir mit dem Hammer und Meißel theils Stufen in die glatten Wände schlugen, theils Löcher machten, unsere vorräthigen Eisen eintrieben" VII, 199). That these measures are not merely a necessary part of the work but a willful attempt to inflict destruction can be seen by the excitement of the men, who sense that they are in mortal combat and express an urge to gain ascendancy over nature, an urge which, according to the author, is basically inherent in man: "Meine Leute wurden immer eifriger. Wie überhaupt der Mensch einen Trieb hat, die Natur zu besiegen und sich zu ihrem Herrn zu machen, was schon die Kinder durch kleines Bauen und Zusammenfügen, noch mehr aber durch Zerstören zeigen" (VII, 199). Heinrich, too, reveals his desire to master nature, not only by striking blows at the rocks, but by risking his life, as do the mountain-dwellers, in order to "conquer" the mountains ("zu zähmen...zu besteigen, zu überwinden" VII, 199).

On the summit of the highest peak Heinrich experiences the ultimate form of isolation. With the sky empty, endless, and dark above him ("der Himmel...in der dunkelblauen Finsternis hin eine endlosere Wüste" VII, 200), he perceives the illusoriness of the world and of existence itself: "Alles schwieg unter mir, als wäre die Welt ausgestorben, als wäre Das, daß sich Alles von Leben rege und rühre, ein Traum gewesen" (VII, 200). As he looks down, he sees no trace of the city or of life. There is absolute silence beneath him, as if the world had been wiped out, as if, in fact, it had never existed.

In the mountain episode, which began with a feeling of vague distress, Heinrich was led to an awareness of death and of nature's hostility. On the summit he gains insight into the fundamental unreality of existence, into the nothingness beyond concrete physical nature. Face to face with the absolute void, Heinrich's isolation takes on the measure of infinity and his being is in utmost peril.

As Risach once looked down from a precipice and felt the desolation of his life, so Heinrich gazes down into an abyss of nothingness and senses the utter desolation of man in the universe. Risach did not commit suicide because of the memory of his mother; neither does Heinrich yield to the threat of annihilation nor succumb to nihilism. At this moment of crisis he turns his thoughts to human beings who are precious to him, mentioning each one in turn: "Alle,... die mir theuer waren, Vater, Mutter und Schwester ... mein lieber Gastfreund ... die gute, klare Mathilde ... Eustach ... der fröhliche, feurige Gustav ... Nataliens Augen" (VII, 200). The descriptive adjectives used with Mathilde and Gustav show Heinrich lingering nostalgically upon the members of Natalie's family, as his thoughts lead finally to the contemplation of his beloved's eyes. Here too, as in the case of Risach, love is shown to be the power that saves man from the forces of destruction.

The mountain experience has been a profoundly moving one for all the men, and its gravity becomes imprinted upon their faces: "so zeigte sich in dem Ernste von Kaspars harten Zügen oder in den Angesichtern der andern ... eine gewisse Veränderung" (VII, 201). In Heinrich, too, a change has taken place. Where formerly he was a mere collector of data, now he becomes a philosopher-scientist who speculates upon the causes and origins of phenomena. More important, however, is the change that has taken place in his heart: he has developed an increased capacity for love, which shows itself immediately upon his next meeting with Risach: "Der Empfang war beinahe bewegt, wie zwischen einem Vater und einem Sohne, so sehr war meine Liebe zu ihm schon gewachsen" (VII, 203), and in his deepened appreciation of Mathilde's loveliness: "Ihr Angesicht war so heiter und freundlich, daß ich meinte, es nie so gesehen zu haben" (VII, 203).

In the presence of the marble muse Heinrich learns to appreciate beauty; in the desolation of the mountains he acquires human warmth. Where the revelation of the marble muse heralds Heinrich's aesthetic maturation, the revelation upon the mountain signifies his emotional completion. Both experiences are necessary to make him worthy of Natalie's hand in marriage.

Einsamkeit is present in *Der Nachsommer* because the characters have an inner life of the soul which is separate and alone. In addition, these persons, who are dedicated to the highest ideals, are resigned to a relative isolation from worldly society for the sake of maintaining their ideals and preserving them for the future. When such human beings meet and achieve a harmonious relationship, the sting of isolation is removed and joy takes its place.

Though in *Der Nachsommer*, as in the season itself, light predominates, shadows are also there, giving depth and spiritual dimension to the characters. While Heinrich's attainment of full and perfect manhood is the goal of the action, death, the extreme form of solitude, is also woven into the world of *Der Nachsommer*, for awareness of death is essential to maturity. The malignant forces in nature and the insignificance of man in the face of the universe are problems not ignored in the novel. The threat of annihilation has here, however, no final dominion over the man with a capacity for love.[15]

III

MATHILDE AND THE ROSES

Among the early reactions to Stifter's *Der Nachsommer*, one year after its publication, was Hebbel's derisive criticism of the detailed and exhaustive description of objects in the novel.[1] Hebbel's criticism was unkind, but superficially pertinent, because description does indeed abound in *Der Nachsommer*. However, the mass of detail that he ridiculed is precisely a source of fascination for modern scholars, who seize upon the number of objects as the distinguishing characteristic of this novel and accord it high esteem because of the very significance of the "things" in it. Far from being extraneous elements, as Hebbel regarded them, the art and nature objects provide both a rich setting of beauty and a mirror-background to the human story in the foreground.

The symbol in *Der Nachsommer* which contrasts most sharply with the austere beauty of the primary symbol, the marble muse, but which is almost as important, is that of the rose.[2] The roses of the novel fulfill many functions. Most strikingly they become a symbol of the other heroine in the novel, Mathilde, identified with her as closely as the muse is identified with Natalie. The roses also serve to express the author's views on the relationship between nature and art; they appear in the background of the Risach-Mathilde love story, suggesting its true emotional quality; they provide the spiritual link between the failure of the older couple and the success of the younger. An examination of their expository function and symbolic content reveals subtleties of plot, characterization, and the author's intentions.

The roses are first introduced in their most realistic aspect as plants which must be tended with great care. Heinrich is so impressed by the wall of roses surrounding Risach's house, and by the extraordinary attention given to its cultivation, that he calls the home of the elderly gentleman "Rosenhaus." No effort had been made to bring about a special color scheme; the only intention apparent in the arrangement of the rose bushes was the construction of an uninterrupted, continuous wall of roses (VI, 45).[3] The importance that Risach attaches to the "wholeness" of the wall is stressed.[4] The creation of the unbroken rose wall is like the creation of a work of art. No effort is spared to bring it to perfection. Risach collects rose compost from a wide area to provide soil for the roses; he builds a shelter to protect them from winter winds and attaches a linen screen to the house to filter out extreme sunlight; he places an irrigating device on the roof of the house so that the roses can be watered from above; and finally, he goes to a great deal of trouble to attract birds to keep the flowers free from insects. Everything is done to enhance the splendor of the roses: their location causes the sun to glorify them; the white wall above and the white sand in front intensify their color; the lawn around the sand resembles a green velvet ribbon. Man, working in harmony with nature, has produced here in the perfect, unbroken wall of roses a work of art that shows characteristics inherent in all works of art.[5]

The care which Risach accords the roses, and the human terms he uses in speaking of them, indicate that in *Der Nachsommer* everything, no matter how trivial it may seem by common standards, has value.[6] Risach refines the wild rose, originally a pleasant but common flower (VI, 253), as he refines Heinrich. "Ihr," says Heinrich's father to Risach, "habt ihn gebildet und *veredelt*" (VIII, 213). Heinrich's development from an ordinary middle-class youth to an extraordinary young man is effected and accelerated in the stimulating atmosphere of the *Rosenhaus*, where the roses, too, bloom earlier and more gloriously than elsewhere.

Mathilde's close relationship to the roses has many facets. Her room in the *Rosenhaus* is called "Rosenzimmer" because its color scheme is similar to that of the rose wall (VI, 184 f.). Risach's simile that likened the vigor of healthy but fading roses to the charm of once beautiful elderly women comes to Heinrich's mind when he meets Mathilde: "Als ich Mathilden das erste Mal sah, fiel mir das Bild der verblühenden Rose ein, welches mein Gastfreund *von ihr* gebraucht hatte" (VII, 176). "Verblüht" and "abgeblüht," words usually applied to faded flowers, describe the Mathilde Heinrich knows. Just as faded roses still show traces of former glory, so does Mathilde's face with its marks of past suffering reflect a heaven of past beauty (VIII, 166), a beauty that was once even finer than that of roses (VIII, 127). Mathilde is often seen at the wall of roses, arranging the blooms, picking out the dead leaves, separating crowded branches. Occasionally she stands there silently, in an attitude of contemplation (VI, 292). Whenever she appears, roses are present. The loveliest roses of the garden are placed in her room; she puts a rose on the table to be her companion while she reads; during a farewell scene, faded rose petals blow about her feet. The rose is her flower, her symbol, she is a rose: "Ueber die vielen feinen Fältchen war ein so sanftes und zartes Roth, daß man sie lieben mußte, und daß sie *eine Rose dieses Hauses* war, die im Verblühen noch schöner sind, als andere Rosen in ihrer vollen Blüthe" (VI, 260 f.).

During the formal rose celebration the roses seem to flower in the realm of myth. Realism is here discarded as we move gradually and almost imperceptibly to the plane of the transcendental. The first emotional tension is felt in the description of the "thousands" of roses almost ready to burst into bloom ("Tausende harrten des Augenblicks, in dem sie aufbrechen würden" VI, 259). Risach, delighted that Mathilde has arrived in time, expresses his feeling of suspense with restrained excitement: "Keine einzige der Rosen ist noch aufgebrochen; aber alle sind bereit dazu" (VI, 266). After Risach's workmen bring an armchair outside to face the rose wall, Mathilde seats herself, while her friends and relatives stand in a group around her. Referred to only as "die Frau" in this scene, Mathilde is depersonalized. "The lady" is the focal point of the ritual in which everyone silently contemplates the roses:

> Die Frau setzte sich in den Sessel, legte die Hände in den Schoß und betrachtete die Rosen.

> Wir standen um sie. Natalie stand zu ihrer Linken, neben
> dieser Gustav, mein Gastfreund stand hinter dem Stuhle, und
> ich stellte mich ... an die rechte Seite und etwas weiter zurück.
> Nachdem die Frau eine ziemliche Zeit gesessen war, stand
> sie schweigend auf, und wir verließen den Platz. (VI, 266 f.)

The lady in the center of this living tableau transcends the human and takes on the aspect of the Madonna, whose flower by tradition is the rose. Like the *mater dolorosa*, Mathilde has suffered and, having made a sacrifice of her life, she is now in a state of grace.[7] With the "lady of forgivingness" dominating the rose-ritual, it becomes a commemoration of love and suffering with Christian overtones. Finally the height of the season is reached:

> Unter dem *klarsten, schönsten* und *tiefsten* Blau des Himmels
> standen nun eines Tages *Tausende* von den Blumen *offen*, es
> schien, daß keine einzige Knospe im Rückstande geblieben und
> nicht aufgegangen ist. In ihrer Farbe von dem reinsten Weiß
> in gelbliches Weiß, in Gelb, in blasses Roth, in feuriges
> Rosenroth, in Purpur, in Veilchenroth, in Schwarzroth, zogen
> sie an der Fläche dahin, daß man *bei lebendiger Anschauung*
> versucht wurde, jenen alten Völkern Recht zu geben, die die
> Rosen fast *göttlich verehrten* und bei ihren Freuden und Festen
> sich mit diesen Blumen bekränzten. (VI, 290)

The blue of the sky is described in superlatives; the number of roses blooming surpasses rational human calculation; the perfection of the flowering is absolute.[8] The flowers are "open" to the blue of heaven, and the colors are listed in rapturous declamation, as Heinrich seems to linger deliberately in delight of them. The puzzling phrase "bei lebendiger Anschauung," standing as it does between such ecstatic description and a reference to divine worship, suggests that this is no mere contemplation of roses, but the beatific vision, a *contemplatio dei*.

In order to understand why the roses mean so much to Mathilde and why they inspire such admiration, awe, and even worship at the *Rosenhaus,* one must examine the role they play in the youthful love affair between Risach and Mathilde.

As a very young man Risach takes a position as tutor and companion to a little boy, Alfred, and his fourteen-year-old sister, Mathilde. Much time is spent at the country estate of the Maklodens, where the children study nature out-of-doors and enjoy the lovely garden and the hexagonal garden house with its rose-covered walls.

After a year of companionship, Risach and Mathilde suddenly discover that they are in love with each other. Their increasingly ardent attachment is kept secret from everyone else, until Risach's guilty conscience drives him to inform Mrs. Makloden, with Mathilde's permission. Mrs. Makloden reacts to the confession with sorrow. Since Risach must first establish himself in a profession, and Mathilde at fifteen must be free to spend several years more in study and preparation for marriage, the association between the two, she feels, had best be discontinued at this time, so as not to hinder their development by placing them under a severe emotional strain during a long period of waiting. Mrs. Makloden appeals to Risach's esteem for her daughter in asking that he leave their home and renounce Mathilde, at least for the present. Emotionally unconvinced, Risach nevertheless accepts Mrs. Makloden's judgment and tells Mathilde of her mother's request. Mathilde interprets his ready acquiescence as a betrayal of their love. When Risach departs, he despairs of ever possessing Mathilde, for she has lost all faith in him. Some years later, when he is in a position to propose marriage to any girl of high social standing, his indirect overtures to Mathilde are met with unmistakable signs of her contempt for him. Risach and Mathilde each marry someone else, but in both cases the marriages are without real love and happiness. Eventually, as widower and widow, they meet again and spend the late years of their lives together in friendship.

This story of frustration, suffering, and failure stands in marked contrast to the otherwise almost unblemished *Nachsommer*-world. Only through the details of its stylistic presentation and its symbolism can its meaning be understood and its function in the novel be divined. The tragic outcome of the love affair is not brought about by the unreasonableness of the parents nor by an innocent misunderstanding between the lovers. It is instead the inevitable result of Risach's awkward and immoral behavior and of Mathilde's excessively romantic attitude.

In the narrative, Mathilde is introduced as not yet grown up. She is described as "halberwachsen" and called "Kind," her immaturity symbolized by the wild ducks of the pond who swim close to their mother because they are not yet able to fly.[9] Mathilde's physical and spiritual purity is emphasized by the stress on her immaculate appearance: "man hielt sie sehr *rein*. Ihre Kleider mußten immer *ohne Makel* sein, ihre Zähne, ihre Hände mußten sehr *rein* sein, und ihr Haupt und ihre Haare wurden täglich so vortrefflich geordnet, daß *kein Tadel* entstehen konnte" (p. 123). It is Risach's responsibility to keep her away from swampy or dirty places: "Ich hatte nur den Auftrag zu sorgen, ... daß sie nicht in sumpfige oder unreine Gegenden komme" (p. 123). Mathilde is cherished by her parents as something very precious which must be protected from any harsh force, as illustrated by the clothing she wears on a journey: a dark wool dress that covers the tips of her shoes, a coat which hides ("verhüllte") the upper part of her body up to the chin, a warm, well-lined hat whose sides caress ("sich wohl anschmiegten" p. 124) her cheeks.

At first the relationship among the three children is clear and untroubled. A disturbance is noted when Mathilde stands apart from other children and watches their play without interest ("theilnahmslos"). Risach's sudden question with the impermissible "du" form, "Mathilde, liebst Du denn auch mich?" releases her feeling for him. As she flies into his arms, the adjectives describing the embrace ("die *sanften* Lippen, die *jungen* Arme, ... die *schlanke* Gestalt" p. 130) stress her youthful fragility. Risach, who had previously been enjoined to protect this child from violence ("keine heftigen Bewegungen" p. 123), presses her so violently ("so heftig" p. 130) against him that she sighs and trembles. This transgression is metaphorically repeated when he breaks off a "tender" rose twig to give to his beloved, although he knows it is actually forbidden to do so ("Ich knickte einen zarten Zweig, *was eigentlich nicht erlaubt war*, und

25

gab ihr den Zweig" p. 134). Though to us the breaking off of a rose twig would seem to have little moral significance, the act here signifies a breaking of the rules and must be considered symbolically as a transgression against the moral code. There is another interesting use of this symbol — the plucking of a rose as indicative of a moral flaw — in connection with Heinrich's sister.[10] In the high standards set for the society in *Der Nachsommer* any deviation from strictly ethical behavior is a sin, an outward manifestation of an inner defect. The violation of the rose has the same meaning as the ravishment of Mathilde: both actions indicate a fault in Risach.

The two young people do not feel at ease with each other after their embrace. Mathilde blushes "in unsäglicher Scham" (p. 130), and Risach feels "beklommen" (p. 131). Immediately after their avowal of eternal love, they receive through Alfred's observations on the condition of things in the garden a fateful warning. As if reminding them to guard their good name, he points out how easily the name plates of the trees become sullied if people are not careful. He has also found apples that are spoiled because they ripened prematurely through an insect bite. Others, fallen too soon from trees too heavily laden, are likewise going to waste. Offering the admonition against premature and excessive emotion, the nature imagery further suggests the proper attitude for the lovers to assume. Alfred speaks of the harvest time, soon to come, when even the grape (symbol of fertility and intoxication) will be ripe. He looks forward to it with joy and entreats them to be patient: "Es sei gar nicht mehr lange bis dahin" (p. 132). The young people do not heed him; they pay no attention to the law of gradual ripening as operative in external nature, but rush headlong into a premature relationship involving secrecy and guilt.

Risach commits an impropriety and reveals his guilty conscience when he fails to visit Mathilde's mother on the afternoon of the garden incident. Hoping for another glimpse of Mathilde, he strays aimlessly ("schweifte" p. 132) through the bushes. He does not answer Mrs. Makloden's question about his absence. Rejecting this opportunity to confess to her, Risach also withholds his confidence from Mr. Makloden, who had asked to be regarded as an older brother. Anxious from the beginning of his employment with this family that no distrust should arise between himself and his employers, Risach now thoughtlessly betrays their trust.

The relationship between Risach and Mathilde is clandestine and exclusive. Their vows of love express with almost pathological intensity the desire for eternal involvement with each other alone: "'Mathilde, Dein auf immer und auf ewig, nur Dein allein, und nur Dein, nur Dein allein!' 'O ewig Dein, ewig, ewig, Gustav, Dein, nur Dein, und nur Dein allein!'" (p. 137). In the company of others Mathilde is apathetic, aloof, indifferent: "So war Mathilde... theilnahmsloser als je. Sie hielt sich ferne, wie Eine, die nicht hieher gehört" (p. 138). Risach knows that her whole being with all its marvelous qualities ("sie mit ihrer wundervollen Gestalt, mit der Wärme ihrer Seele und dem Glanz ihres Aufblühens" p. 139) belongs only to him, and she is aware of his deification ("Vergötterung" p. 139) of her.

Throughout the interlude Mathilde yields unquestioningly to her emotions, whereas Risach, older and in a position of responsibility, voices apprehension: "Wie wird das werden, o, wie wird das werden?!" (p. 140). Once, when he meets Mrs. Makloden's glance after furtively kissing Mathilde, he is so disturbed that he cancels his plan to visit a friend that afternoon. When he finally acknowledges his guilt to himself, it horrifies him. He perceives it like worms or rodents in his happiness ("bohrte,... nagte" p. 142); it assumes the magnitude of Greek tragedy: "Es war wie das Unheil der Alten, welches immer größer wird, wenn man es berührt" (p. 142).

By the very fact of its concealment, the emotion between Risach and Mathilde takes on a threatening character: "Je tiefer sich das Gefühl verbergen mußte, desto *gewaltiger* war es, desto *drängender loderte* es in dem Innern" (p. 136). The extravagance of their feeling is expressed in superlatives and in the vocabulary of romantic literature: Mathilde is "so schön wie ein Engel," like the stem of a heavenly lily "zaubervoll," "anmuthsvoll," "unbegreiflich" (p. 135), "das Wesen,... das von überirdischen Räumen war, meine Seele zu erfüllen" (p. 139). He calls her "du himmelvolles Wesen"; she calls him "der Trefflichste von Allen, ...König, der Einzige" (p. 140). Their wealth in possessing each other is "ein unermeßlicher" (p. 137). The romantic art of music is drawn upon to reflect the intensity of Mathilde's feelings. In the grip of passion she loses control of herself, playing the zither as if she can never stop ("Die Saiten mußten sie so ergriffen haben, daß sie nicht aufhören konnte" p. 136). Risach loses all sense of rational values and proportion. He adores Mathilde to such a degree that the whole universe is as nothing beside her: "Es ist nicht zu sagen, woher es kommt, daß vor einem Herzen die Erde, der Himmel, die Sterne, die Sonne, *das ganze Weltall verschwindet*" (p. 135) — an extreme expression of romantic love indeed!

The figures of speech employed throughout the episode suggest the violence of the emotion which has come over Risach "wie ein Sturmwind" (p. 132). The sight of his beloved strikes him like a flash of lightning (p. 133); she stands before him as "eine feurige Flamme" (p. 134). The secret of their love is like "Glut im Herzen" (p. 133). The cliché of "burning passion" recurs as Mathilde is described as "dunkelglühend," and their embrace "ein glühender Kuß" (p. 140).

The language of *Der Nachsommer*, otherwise consistently classical in its calm dignity,[11] assumes in this episode characteristically romantic qualities, reminiscent of an earlier, younger Stifter.[12] Abounding in violence, extravagance, overstatement, and even cliché, the stylistic tone of this episode is in as questionable taste as the behavior of Risach and Mathilde is indiscreet. Their lack of emotional control is reflected in their unrestrained verbal expressions. Carried away by a passion that may be called "demonic,"[13] the young people forget themselves and their place in society. The very boundlessness of their feeling prevents them from giving their relationship a form viable within their social situation.[14] In its excessive and exclusive preoccupation with itself, the relationship fails to achieve that radiance common to all perfect things in *Der Nachsommer*; out of harmony with its surroundings, it fails to emit any beneficent force and thus becomes as empty to itself as it is sterile to the world outside.[15]

The lovers feel that their relationship, which is based on a formless and socially unsanctioned covenant between them, is sufficient to itself and self-sustaining. Their intense focus upon themselves and their romantic feelings blurs their perception of the world outside.[16] The discrepancy between reality as they experience it and the true nature of their situation is illustrated by the garden house, where the roses seem to them to be blooming, but actually are not.[17] The discrepancy between perception and fact is shown again when Risach mistakes the sunset reflection on Mathilde's window-pane for the rosy glow of her face, "aber es war nur ein schiefes Hereinleuchten der beginnenden Abendröthe gewesen" (p. 132). The word "schief" adds a critical commentary to the romance, and the sunset forebodes its end. The outside world, in the form of Mathilde's mother, finally intrudes upon the idyll. Faced with her consternation, Risach becomes aware of the difference between what he experienced and what is real, at least to the parents ("Wir haben uns nicht vorzustellen vermocht, daß Das, was für uns ein so *hohes Glück* war, für die Eltern ein *Unheil* sein wird" p. 149). Mrs. Makloden explains that a secret love pact is not a sufficient foundation for an acceptable union, when emotional and moral maturity and the educational background required for the establishment of a family are lacking.

She feels some responsibility for the course of events, because she and her husband had trusted Risach too much. The faltering of her voice on the word "trust" ("Ich habe Euch so — so sehr vertraut" p. 143) shows how deeply she has been affected by his betrayal. Only in reference to the tardiness of his confession, "welches freilich etwas früher hätte gemacht werden sollen" (p. 145), does she blame Risach; otherwise her appraisal of the situation is objective, fair, and benevolent. Reassuring Risach of her continued affection, she calls him "son" and promises that later, when he is in a position to marry, she will give him and Mathilde her blessings.

Risach's response is an outcry of distress at the loss he must suffer: "Jetzt bin ich ganz allein" (p. 147). Engrossed in his own anguish,[18] he does not perceive the intimation that separation from Mathilde need be only temporary. Obtusely ignoring the mother's kindness and wisdom, he hears in bitterness only the categorical imperative that a child must obey its parents. Rejecting a reasonable view of a complicated and delicate matter, Risach gives himself a crass summation of Mrs. Makloden's advice: he must sever connections with Mathilde because her parents insist upon it.

Nowhere is Risach's awkwardness more devastating than in the scene in which he conveys to Mathilde the decision of her parents. Although he intended to tell her gently ("ich wollte Dir das Nothwendige recht sanft und weich sagen" p. 154), his voice trembles and his breath fails. Without giving any reasons, Risach repeats only his own stern dictum that parents must be obeyed ("Ich ging auf die Gründe, welche die Mutter angegeben hatte, nicht ein und legte Mathilden nur dar, daß sie zu gehorchen habe, und daß unter Ungehorsam unser Bund nicht bestehen könne" p. 151). This blunt command, issued without endearment or any mitigating explanation, without regard for the sensitive nature of Mathilde, strikes with brutal impact.

Stunned, Mathilde asks him to repeat what he has said, and again he can only answer that she must do the will of her parents. Now, with all the intensity of her being, Mathilde denounces Risach for having broken the bond between them without consulting her.[19] His love that has yielded so readily to parental demands seems paltry to her beside her own proud and complete surrender to love. Too late Risach seeks to justify her mother's position and his own behavior. Anger and bewilderment block Mathilde's understanding, as pain and self-pity had blocked Risach's. Judging the demands of love higher than those of "duty," she insists that it should have been impossible for him to give her up. She feels that in thus "breaking faith" with her, he has destroyed the magic of a love that she had held to be eternal. Bereft of her faith in Risach and his love, she is plunged into confusion and despair, with nothing to sustain her. The foundation of her world is shattered, and she is threatened with chaos:

> Deine Liebe ist nicht die, die ich dachte, und die die meinige ist. Ich habe den Vergleichspunkt verloren und weiß nicht, wie Alles ist. Wenn Du einst gesagt hättest, der Himmel ist nicht der Himmel, die Erde nicht die Erde, ich hätte es Dir

> geglaubt. Jetzt weiß ich es nicht, ob ich Dir glauben soll, was
> Du sagst. Ich kann nicht anders, ich weiß es nicht, und ich
> kann nicht machen, daß ich es weiß. O Gott! daß es geworden
> ist, wie es ward, und daß zerstörbar ist, was ich für ewig hielt!
> wie werde ich es ertragen können? (p. 155)

The roses, always in the background of the love story, come into prominence at the end. Risach's conversation with the mother takes place in the rose season ("da eben die Rosenblüthe war" p. 142). The young couple sit in the shadows of a rosebush on a bench, "auf welche von einem Rosengebüsche Schatten fiel" (p. 150), while the shadows fall over their romance. The phrase describing the garden house, "an dem die Rosen blühten," occurs twice and sounds the concluding cadence. It is to the roses that Mathilde kneels down, as to a Deity, invoking them to be witness of her ineffable love: "Hört es, Ihr tausend Blumen, die herab schauten, als er diese Lippen küßte, ... ich habe ihn geliebt, wie es mit keiner Zunge in keiner Sprache ausgesprochen werden kann" (p. 153). As she buries her face in the roses, Risach again notes her similarity to the flowers: "Ihre glühende Wange war auch jetzt noch schöner, als die Rosen" (p. 155). She draws convulsively away from his attempted caress, and he, powerless to console her, shows his anguish by grasping the thorny branches until his blood streams down the rosebushes.

The romance which began with a forbidden embrace ends with a broken heart: "In der Pflicht," says Risach, "bricht mein Herz, und in dem brechenden Herzen bist Du" (p. 154). Mathilde does not notice his bleeding hands. After she has gained her composure, he makes no further attempt to reach her, for he feels that her anger shields her from further grief.

Many years later, when Risach has acquired an estate and developed a rose wall around his own house, the aging Mathilde returns to him. She stands in front of the roses and with tears streaming down her face asks forgiveness. He declares that her fault was no greater than his: "Dein schmerzhaftes Zürnen war die Liebe, und mein schmerzhaftes Zurückhalten war auch die Liebe" (p. 167). Looking upon the roses around Risach's house as a sign of his continued affection, Mathilde would interpret the coincidence of her arrival during the rose season as a judgment against her ("ein Strafgericht" p. 167), but Risach directs her thoughts away from past sorrows by offering to help her in the present. Mathilde puts her son under his guidance and, with her daughter, regularly visits the *Rosenhaus* whenever the roses bloom. At Risach's suggestion that he will remove the roses if they recall painful memories, she protests that they are a lovely adornment to the house and have become the most precious thing in her life ("das Theuerste" p. 170). The roses now symbolize their separation and reunion: "Merkmal unserer Trennung und Vereinigung" (p. 171).

The relationship between Risach and Mathilde no longer has the character of glorious, red roses; it has gone beyond passion "zu einem edlen, tiefen, freundlichen Gefühle" (p. 170). Yet when Mathilde refers to the faded roses as symbols of their faded happiness, Risach rejects the symbol by gently correcting her:

> In diesem Augenblicke ertönte...Mathildens Stimme, die sagte: "Wie diese Rosen abgeblüht sind, so ist unser Glück abgeblüht."
> Ihr antwortete die Stimme meines Gastfreundes, welche sagte: "Es ist nicht abgeblüht, es hat nur eine andere Gestalt." (VII, 126 f.)[20]

The youthful love, which was cut off, has been transfigured into a Platonic friendship[21]: "stille, durchaus aufrichtige, süße Freundschaft,...die über alles Lob und über allen Tadel erhaben ist, und die vielleicht das Spiegelklarste ist, was menschliche Verhältnisse aufzuweisen haben" (VIII, 172). The bond between them, transcending the purely natural ("hat gleichsam keinen irdischen Ursprung an sich" VIII, 172), has been transmuted into a *Gestalt* of unchanging beauty.

The circumstances surrounding their conversation reveal a new symbol. Heinrich, inside the house, inadvertently overhears it while sketching the iron window shutters. At the moment when the voices reach him he is contemplating a marvellous rose, delicately wrought of iron, in the center of the shutters.[22] This rose, no longer subject to change or decay as are the roses of nature, illustrates the *Gestalt* of the late friendship between Risach and Mathilde in a permanent art figure.

Indirectly, even the consummate manifestation of love as it develops between Heinrich and Natalie is a product of the injury suffered by their elders, who in their painfully acquired wisdom were able to provide the young people with the right kind of education.[23] Natalie as a child, with the same black eyes and the same brown hair as her mother, strongly resembles Mathilde at the same age: "Eine größere Gleichheit... kann nicht mehr gedacht werden" (VIII, 170), and one would assume that her emotional make-up too is similar to Mathilde's. However, although Natalie is as beautiful as her mother, she is never once compared to a rose, for her character shows none of the romantic abandon so calamitous for Mathilde. Instead, she has been given early, through education, strength of character and a noble spirit.[24] Her being is classical in its balance as her appearance is classical in a form like that of Greek maidens.[25]

Both Risach and Mathilde are concerned that Natalie shall find happiness in marriage. The terms "affection" ("Neigung") and "high regard" ("Hochachtung" VIII, 173) are used by Risach to indicate the felicitous love that can bring this about. Indeed the sentiment between Heinrich and Natalie does have a different quality from that between young Risach and Mathilde. Love does not suddenly overwhelm them with the power of thousands of red roses bursting into bloom; rather it becomes clear to them gradually — like marble, which seems almost transparent when one gazes deeply into it (VII, 275). In what is perhaps the strangest and most chastely beautiful love scene in literature, the couple calmly and reverently discourse about the most wonderful things they know: water, jewels, works of art. Especially extolled is white marble for its purity, perfection, beauty, depth, and transparency. The transfiguration of the world that Heinrich experiences when he looks through a thin slice of marble ("Dann scheint die Welt fast goldartig, wenn man sie durch ihn ansieht" VII, 276), is likewise experienced when he views the world through the eyes of love: "Wie hatte seit einigen Augenblicken Alles sich um mich verändert, und wie hatten die Dinge eine Gestalt gewonnen, die ihnen sonst nicht eigen war" (VII, 284). Marble, this jewel, this "Stoff, ... der keine Makel hat," illustrates the clarity and perfection of ideal love.

In contrast to Mathilde, Natalie does not surrender herself to passion; instead she remains in possession of herself. Without abandoning self-esteem, she is as fond of Heinrich as of her own life ("wie meinem Leben" VII, 281). Her regard for him is rationally founded on a recognition of his human worth: "Da liebe ich Euch, *weil* Ihr so einfach, so gut, und doch so ernst seid" (VII, 283). Heinrich does not adore Natalie to the exclusion of everyone else; rather he includes her in that circle of persons who mean much to him — though she means more to him than the others (VII, 282). They vow eternal devotion to each other, but respect their parents' right to give or deny them permission to marry. They immediately inform their parents of their engagement and receive unhesitating blessings.

Whereas the young Mathilde once exclaimed in bitterness: "Es ist Alles vorüber" (VIII, 156), Natalie exclaims in joy and wonderment: "Nun ist doch erfüllet, was sich vorbereitete" (VII, 287). During his first visit to the *Rosenhaus* Heinrich perceived the fragrance of the roses as a sacrificial offering: "Der Duft von den Tausenden der Rosen stieg wie eine Opfergabe zu mir empor" (VI, 79 f.). It is the roses which link broken love with blessed love. Devotion to the roses in *Der Nachsommer* is devotion to love.[26] The suffering offered like a sacrifice by Risach and Mathilde is redeemed by Heinrich and Natalie in a glorious consummation. The last rose season in the novel is celebrated as a memorial of both the past and the future: "Die Zeit der Rosenblüthe was heran gerückt, und heuer sollte sie von den vereinigten Familien als ein *Denkzeichen der Vergangenheit* und aber auch als eins der Zukunft zum ersten Male in dieser Vereinigung und mit besonderer Festlichkeit begangen werden" (VIII, 234).

The roses of *Der Nachsommer* appear in many different contexts and have diverse functions. In Risach's unbroken rose wall, the fulfillment of a perfect *Gestalt* is their purpose and illustrative achievement. As a symbol for Mathilde they show first her glowing vitality and later the charm and vigor of her fading years. So close is the spiritual association between her and the roses that the service she renders them reveals her own essential qualities of renunciation, loving kindness, and forgivingness, qualities which in the rose ritual seem to reach mystical dimensions. In the garden at Heinbach the roses are witness to the love affair of Risach and Mathilde, reflecting the intensity of their passion and the extravagance of their romanticism. In the "temple" of the rose-covered garden house the young people experience ecstacy; in front of the roses Mathilde suffers the shattering of her world and Risach the mortification of his flesh. Though the author indicates his disapproval of such self-abandonment to passion by confronting young Risach with a suicidal abyss, the image of the rose itself is never abandoned. The last rose celebration coincides with the wedding of Heinrich and Natalie. In linking the past with the future, the rose on this occasion symbolizes redemption of past error and suffering and the promise of a joyous future.

In *Der Nachsommer*, as in every great work of literature, the dualism between the classic and the romantic is resolved. Natalie, who displays perfect form and calm dignity, and Mathilde, who first expresses rapturous yearning and later mystical renunciation, embody the polarity of the two concepts, yet are harmoniously related as daughter and mother. While it is Natalie to whom the author accords highest honor and admiration, it is Mathilde who most deeply touches the heart. The Greek *Marmorgestalt* representing Natalie stands in the center of the novel and from there its presence radiates in both directions; the roses evoking Mathilde and her love affair twine through the novel and encircle it from beginning to end. Thus the symbol of the classic and the symbol of the romantic, marble statue and rose, are held in extraordinary and exquisite balance.[27]

IV

THE *CEREUS PERUVIANUS*: ILLUSTRATION OF A *GESTALT*

Risach, the sage and mentor in Stifter's *Der Nachsommer*, at one point rejects Heinrich's evaluation of things as "great" or "trivial" by pointing out that all things together bring fulfillment to man's life: "Es gehört wohl Beides und Alles zu dem Ganzen, daß sich das Leben erfülle und beglücke (VI, 235).[1] Since Risach consistently functions as spokesman for Stifter's own philosophy, one can assume that the author endowed each of the many things in the novel with value. The notoriously lengthy descriptions in *Der Nachsommer* do not constitute pedantry on the part of the author, but rather mark the significance of all, even seemingly trivial items, to the totality of the novel. The thesis that individual things, great and small, have value is programmatic for *Der Nachsommer*; every single entity presented has intrinsic merit as well as pertinence to the story of Heinrich's development.

It has been demonstrated that the marble statue, the most striking object in *Der Nachsommer*, functions as a gauge for Heinrich's development and a vehicle for the author's philosophy. Although a comprehensive study of all the objects in *Der Nachsommer* would be required to gain full understanding of the nature of the novel's world and the meaning of the events in it, close examination of one of the minor objects will microcosmically reveal the basic design of the work. The painstaking artistry infused into each object down to its last detail suggests the intensity of Stifter's attention to all of the created "things," and indicates the wide scope of the field in which his aesthetic-ethical principles operate. Each thing, even the least prominent, is animated by the same ethos as the central object, the marble statue.

The cactus plant *Cereus Peruvianus*, one of the apparently minor things standing in the background, and largely ignored by critics of the novel, can be seen to play a role analogous to that of the marble statue. Whereas the marble statue, in its magnificence and in the gravity of its treatment by the author, exhibits most impressively the characteristics of a perfect form, the *Cereus Peruvianus*, in its readily comprehensible simplicity, likewise illustrates perfection of form, though perhaps in a manner less awesome. The story of its development will reveal how consistently the author is concerned with *Gestalt* in all things, even the most humble of the many objects populating *Der Nachsommer*.[2]

At the *Rosenhaus*, where art objects are assiduously collected and fashioned, where thousands of roses are cultivated, where the building and landscape are maintained in an excellent condition, where Heinrich undergoes a process of refinement, there is also a greenhouse containing "thousands of flower-pots" with cacti supervised by Simon the gardener. When Heinrich visits here for the first time he remarks that these plants are indeed worthy of cultivation because they are so special and strange. Simon underlines their exotic quality ("immer merkwürdiger, ... verwunderlich wie Märchen" VI, 141). He also mentions a certain cactus, "probably a *Cereus Peruvianus*," which he would like to have, because it is not properly cared for in its present location at the *Inghof*. He feels that Risach, who collects "so many old things," should add this to his collection.

Soon Heinrich has occasion to visit the Ingheims, who own the cactus. This family is described as "unter den Gebildeten," their home exhibits opulence: "schwere Vorhänge, ... ein großes Empfangszimmer, ... die prachtvollen Polster, ... ein schöner Teppich," and their garden is well-tended "wie viele wohlgehaltene und schöne Gärten" (VI, 296). Nevertheless, certain aspects of the surroundings of the Ingheims indicate that these people are not of the highest caliber. For example, the disrepair into which the original old castle on the estate has fallen ("Beide Theile [towers and walls] beginnen aber oben zu verfallen" VI, 294), and the neglected condition of the original mansion, now abandoned, suggest a lack of reverence for the past. The things mistreated here take a kind of revenge upon their owners. The abandoned mansion, for example, "looking down" at Heinrich like a sinister being ("von den mit Brettern verschlagenen Fenstern *schaut* die Unbewohntheit und Ungastlichkeit herab" VI, 294), creates a first impression of hostility, which the social charm of the Ingheims cannot erase. The ugliness of the decaying old buildings contrasts so unpleasantly with the luxury of the Ingheims' own home that one suspects there is something aesthetically amiss with the persons who live in such disharmony.

The cactus is not mentioned by anyone here, an omission which in itself is revealing, because, as Simon observes, it shows that these people have little regard for it: "sie achten den Cereus nicht, sonst hätten sie ja die Gesellschaft zu ihm hingeführt" (VI, 304). A worthy object in *Der Nachsommer* deserves to be appreciated. Failure of the Ingheims to maintain their old buildings and failure to appreciate the cactus are symptomatic of their moral lassitude and incipient corruption.

Certain that the cactus will never come to flower there, Simon urges Heinrich to persuade Risach that he should acquire it. The first step Heinrich takes toward this end is to visit the *Inghof* again for the purpose of examining the cactus. Heinrich is favorably impressed by it: "es war in Wirklichkeit eine sehr schöne und zu ansehnlicher Größe ausgebildete Pflanze" (VI, 313). The untidy condition of its environment, however, confirms Simon's opinion that here the cactus is not treated properly. It stands in the most neglected corner of the greenhouse; it is isolated from all other cacti; it is hidden from view by flower racks containing other kinds of plants. Surrounding it is a variety of debris: "es lagen Blumenstäbe, Bastbänder, welke Blätter und Dergleichen dort" (VI, 313).

The unworthy condition in which the *Cereus Peruvianus* is kept is analogous to the condition of many other objects which were neglected by the world until Risach retrieved them from destruction and restored them. One example is the fourteenth-century church, which shows many signs of the violence inflicted upon it by the ravages of time and man: "Man hatte Fenster zumauern lassen, ... Stellen ... ausgebrochen und die früheren Ueberdächer mit ihren

Verzierungen weg geschlagen" (VII ,345). Even stronger terms of desecration are used to describe the altar of the church at Kerberg: birds and insects have polluted it, it is exposed to the desiccating heat of the sun, parts of it have fallen down and have been thrown together again haphazardly, and finally, the carved figures of the altar are being eroded by worms (VI, 310). One of Risach's loveliest paintings, a medieval Madonna, is found abandoned in the dust of an old attic, where it has been mutilated by a soldier. Undiscovered, it would have fallen into complete decay. The marble statue itself, found among the rubble of old buildings and odd plaster figures in an Italian amusement park, had to be rescued from oblivion and the destructiveness of children heedlessly playing ball around it. Encased in plaster, its exquisite form is covered by boards from the shoulders down. It is Risach's task to free it, repair it, refinish it, provide the right setting for it, and then to display it. All the works of art subject to such barbarous maltreatment seem to point accusingly at the corruption in the world which allows priceless values to be destroyed. Risach and his helpers perform the ethical act of revitalizing these pieces by restoring them to their original beauty.

The cactus, likewise the victim of negligence at the Ingheims, is rescued by Heinrich, who succeeds in persuading Risach to buy it and place it in Simon's care at the *Asperhof*. Through Heinrich's interest and intercession the cactus is taken out of its unattractive quarters and installed in a worthy setting. In words of a solemnity that initially strike the reader as strange and inappropriate for a plant, Simon extols Heinrich as the savior of the *Cereus*: "Ihr habt den Cereus Peruvianus vom Untergang gerettet" (VIII, 225). From the weighty and almost religious term "vom Untergang gerettet," which connotes deliverance and redemption as well as salvagement, Heinrich (and the reader) is forced to conclude that the cactus has metaphysical worth, that it is as precious as any living soul — or indeed as any *Gestalt*.

At the *Asperhof* the cactus is set up in the greenhouse with other cacti. A glass tower is erected over it, so that it no longer has to stoop, but can grow to full height. Through careful staking and through the benefit of the sun's rays which are skillfully directed at the plant ("durch viele Mühe und Kunst" VII, 340), the cactus begins to thrive and gradually assume the tall and straight form inherent in it. Now for the first time its stature and pleasing appearance impress Heinrich: "Ich hätte nicht gedacht, daß diese Pflanze so groß sei und daß sie sich so schön darstellen würde" (VII, 13).

Like the marble statue under the glass roof, the cactus under the glass tower is dignified by its setting, and it assumes aesthetic importance comparable to that of the work of sculpture. There is little essential difference between this live pillar ("der lebendigen Säule" VII, 340) and the marble statue, which also seems alive. There is no dichotomy in *Der Nachsommer* between nature and art, for man cultivates the objects of nature according to scientific and aesthetic principles and he creates his own art-forms with attention to organic laws, using natural forms as models. Thus nature becomes aesthetic and art natural. The artistry of man and the intrinsic natural vitality of the things combine in a typical *Gestalt*.

As with the roses and trees under cultivation at the *Asperhof*, extraordinary measures are taken to protect the cactus from the influence of harsh elements. Through the application of a special glue on the glass tower, no rain, hail, or snow can penetrate. As with works of art, no effort is spared to bring the cactus to a state of beauty. Eventually its color, which has changed from a sickly yellow to a vivid blue-green, indicates its perfect health.

Since perfection is not sterile in *Der Nachsommer*, but acts creatively upon its surroundings, it is inevitable that the *Cereus Peruvianus* too will bring happiness.[3] The joy which this *Gestalt* radiates is symbolized by the white flower anticipated by Simon: "Wenn es so fortgehe, so könne auch noch die Freude der fabelhaften weißen Blume der lebendigen Säule in dieses Haus kommen" (VII, 340).

Heinrich has already experienced the beneficence of the plant itself on a number of occasions. Once when he is in a state of melancholy, Simon compels him to consider the cactus plant. Though Heinrich is irritated at being interrupted in his gloomy introspection, he does admit that thereby his sadness is alleviated: "Das eine Gute hatte aber die Ansprache des Gärtners für mich, daß sie mich von meinen wehmüthigen und schmerzlichen Gefühlen ein wenig abzog" (VI, 304). On a later occasion Heinrich reacts with less annoyance when Simon interrupts his reveries, and he regards with tolerant amusement Simon's singleminded devotion to the plants: "Er bedachte hierbei nicht, daß etwa meine Gedanken anderswo sein könnten" (VII, 340). On both occasions the gardener urges Heinrich to focus his attention on the things around him rather than upon himself. The contemplation of the forms in the objective world frees Heinrich from his self-pity.

Whenever Heinrich visits the *Asperhof*, even in winter, Simon expects him to pay his respects to the cactus, which from year to year becomes more imposing. After Heinrich's engagement we hear for the first time that he takes great interest ("großen Antheil") in these plants, he listens graciously ("freundlich") to the lengthy discourses of the gardener, and he expresses his admiration for the *Cereus* in much stronger terms: "wirklich eine prachtvolle Pflanze" (VIII, 60). It should be noted that only after Heinrich has achieved inner harmony does he fully enjoy this natural object. Heinrich here demonstrates the truth of Risach's early remark that we can truly appreciate things only when we are in harmony with ourselves (VI, 235).

Heinrich's appreciation of Simon increases along with his enjoyment of the cactus. The first time Heinrich sees the gardener he is struck by his white hair and white clothing ("viel reines Weiß an sich" VI, 121). The young man finds the white outfit ridiculous and proclaims in a patronizing tone that Simon's occupation would seem to be that of cook rather than gardener. When Heinrich on his second visit inquires about everyone he met previously, he asks about the gardener only as an afterthought and with a trace of condescension ("Ich fragte *sogar* nach dem weißen, alten Gärtner" VI, 227). He still finds Simon's attire odd: "Er machte mir ganz genau wieder den nämlichen Eindruck, wie im vergangenen Jahre, als ob er einer ganz anderen Beschäftigung angehörte" (VI, 230). The observation, that Simon has grown even whiter than before, attests to a sharpening of Heinrich's spiritual vision rather than to a difference in Simon, who, in Risach's judgment, no longer undergoes change.[4] Heinrich gradually realizes that the white array gives the gardener and his wife distinction over all the other workers: "Unter allen diesen Leuten hoben sich der Gärtner und die Gärtnerin heraus, welche bloß schneeweiß gingen" (VI, 257). Though the whiteness of Simon's garments cannot be explained realistically, it does convey the inner reality of his being. The immaculate raiment reflects the purity of his inner *Gestalt*.

Simon's hair too is white — whiter even than Risach's. Once when Simon ingenuously relates the whiteness of his hair to the cactus flower, he becomes so abashed by his own audacity that he hastily checks himself. His disconcertion shows in his adding a modifying phrase that does not correspond syntactically with the rest of the sentence: "Wenn ich ihn [den Cereus] hier hätte, so würde er bald so weiß, wie meine Haare, blühen, natürlich viel weißer" (VI 303 f.). The fact is that Simon in his serenity and innocence does indeed resemble a white flower. Simon is the ideal representation of the gardener, who embodies all the devotion and patient effort which this occupation requires. The flawless white of his hair and clothing symbolically reinforces the metaphysical connotations of the gardener image.

Simon, whose attitude toward Heinrich gradually assumes parental character ("beinahe etwas Elternhaftes" VIII, 59), often expresses gratitude to the young man for saving the *Cereus* through his goodness ("durch meine Güte, wie er sich ausdrückte" VII, 340). Eager to bring to fulfillment the cactus plant, which belongs to a species that may bloom one night of the year only, Simon zealously cares for it until on Heinrich's wedding night a glorious flower is finally produced. As if offering Heinrich a valuable wedding gift, Simon proudly proclaims the good tidings of great joy: "Alles Gute belohnt sich und Euch erwartet heute noch eine große Freude" (VIII, 225).[5] Simon's words echoing the announcement of Jesus' Nativity, as made to the shepherds, relates the beautiful white flower to the birth of the Christchild — God's gift of love to man. Blooming on the wedding night as a miraculous blessing, the flower associates Natalie with the grace of Heaven, given to Heinrich who has become worthy.[6] In the greenhouse, where an area has been cleared in front of the cactus, and lamps have been arranged for good viewing, the spectators are in complete agreement as to the magnificence of the flower: "eine große, weiße, prachtvolle, fremdartige Blume. Alles war einstimmig im Lob derselben" (VIII, 226).

Although Freudian terminology cannot be brought to bear upon a work so finely wrought as *Der Nachsommer* without tearing its delicate fabric and detracting from its spiritual essence, the parallel between the flowering of the plant and of love on this wedding night must not be overlooked. The blooming of the cactus may be interpreted as the metaphoric realization of the consummation of love. The color white, prominent already in the betrothal scene, where Heinrich and Natalie discourse upon the beauty of white marble while facing the white grotto-nymph, reflects the absolute purity and chastity of erotic love in its ideal manifestation.[7]

The significance of the *Cereus* is, however, not fully defined by a consideration of its symbolic and associative functions. While it is "a great symbol of life and growth,"[8] its primary significance lies in the fact that it is an entity which is permitted to illustrate inner reality in an ideal outward form. Freed from environmental elements impeding its development, and provided with conditions compatible to its nature, it achieves its highest potential, its optimum *Gestalt*. It is symbolic of the protagonist and related to all the other *Gestalten* of nature and art that are gradually reaching completion.

The meaning of the novel becomes evident from the close examination of any one of the things in it. The author demands that each thing in the novel be, in its way, perfect. In thus fulfilling itself, it unites with all the other *Gestalten* to bring about a world of beauty and joy in abundance. It is Stifter's remarkable achievement that he has in his novel made such a world almost credible.[9]

V

AFFIRMATION OF FORMLESSNESS

The world of *Der Nachsommer* with its bountiful *Gestalten* of nature, art, and humanity is recognized as a veritable apotheosis of the concept *Gestalt*.[1] The roses, the trees, the cacti, as well as the art objects, reach perfection of form and condition at the *Asperhof*, where the men, from Simon the gardener to Risach himself, are all engaged in rendering service to things. The concept *Gestalt* is applied to the orderliness of a room, as when Risach reminds his young guest to place a book back upon the shelf, "damit das Zimmer die ihm zugehörige Gestalt behalte" (VI, 57),[2] as well as to the proper relationship between people: "Es ist nicht abgeblüht," says Risach of the love that once brought happiness to himself and Mathilde, "es hat nur eine andere Gestalt" (VII, 127).

Social intercourse at the *Rosenhaus* is governed by the principles of reason, consideration for others, aesthetic awareness, and good form in all matters. The characters' behavior toward other objects and persons is determined by their respect for the *Gestalt* inherent in everything. In rendering service to the *Gestalt* of others, each person finds his own best form, which is inevitably harmonious, autonomous yet integrated with the environment, bounded by reason, and benign in its influence upon others, thus embodying the classical ideal of goodness and beauty unified.[3]

Where the tendency toward beautiful form constitutes virtue, as in *Der Nachsommer*, formlessness is a vice, as Risach's condemnation of "das Einseitige" and "ein Uebermaß von Wünschen und Begehrungen" (VI, 235) shows. Disregard for proper form and self-abandonment to passion may prevent fulfillment of *Gestalt*, as the tragic ending of the youthful love affair between Risach and Mathilde illustrates.⁴ In this novel we do not expect to find any positive evaluation of formlessness, for all manifestations of irrationality threaten the realization of *Gestalt*, a concept which in terms of the novel has a rational foundation. Consequently, we are startled by the sympathetic, though sketchy, portrayal of a character who, both in his person and his art, is indeed an expression of *Gestaltlosigkeit* with its irrational basis.

Joseph the musician does not fit into the rational order prevailing at the *Rosenhaus*, and as an outsider and a nonconformist he has only a tenuous association with the society there. Because of the infrequency of his appearance in the novel, little attention has been devoted to him, the one noteworthy interpretation being an article by Harry Tucker, Jr., who views Joseph not as a peripheral figure without significance, but as an *"Urbild* of music" with "symbolic value."⁵ Although Joseph lives apart from the *Rosenhaus* society and outside the sphere where balance and measure are criteria of worth, he is distinctly more than an anomaly, for he moves in a realm which, literally and figuratively, is higher than anyone else's. At home in the mountains, he has an incomparable distinction over the other characters. While Heinrich and Risach with their men are servants to art, Joseph is a master, a truly creative artist.

Admired and esteemed for his genius by everyone in the surroundings, Joseph is nevertheless shunted almost out of sight by the author. Stifter's chary treatment of Joseph the musician is ambiguous and puzzling. An encomium offered with such reticence and reluctance by an author to one of his characters presents an interesting paradox. Since Joseph is closely linked to his music, we can perhaps approach the resolution of the paradox by determining what is the essence of music for the author.

In attempting a similar examination, Tucker regrettably fails to evaluate much of the evidence within the novel — notably Risach's statements about music and Natalie's and Mathilde's behavior in regard to music. Instead, in his brief article he attempts to cope with an assortment of extraneous and largely irrelevant material from other authors. Stifter's feeling about music, though ambiguous, cannot be summarized by the statement which Tucker quotes from George

Schoolfield: "[music is] the art which he respected but did not love."[6] Such simplistic formulation is neither meaningful nor accurate.

Whereas in *Der Nachsommer* lengthy discourses are held on the aesthetics of the various arts, the art of music receives little comment and no aesthetic analysis. The status of music is questionable. To be sure, Heinrich's father lauds music as the sole medium in which modern man has produced works of a caliber comparable to that of Greek sculpture:

> Das, was die Griechen in der Bildnerei geschaffen haben, ist das Schönste, welches auf der Welt besteht, nichts kann ihm in andern Künsten und in späteren Zeiten an Einfachheit, Größe und Richtigkeit an die Seite gesetzt werden, *es wäre denn in der Musik*, in der wir in der That einzelne Satzstücke, und vielleicht ganze Werke, haben, die der antiken *Schlichtheit* und *Größe* verglichen werden können. Das haben aber Menschen hervor gebracht, deren Lebensbildung auch einfach und antik gewesen ist, ich will nur Bach, Händel, Haydn, Mozart nennen. (VII, 169 f.)

Nevertheless, Drendorf avoids saying anything specific about music; he focuses instead upon certain composers and their supposedly simple and classically great form of life. Neither the composers nor their works are mentioned again, while extensive analyses are given to particular examples of sculpture, painting, and literature.

Risach pointedly and emphatically disclaims any talent for music: "Wenn ein künstlerisches Gestaltungsvermögen in mir war, so war es das eines Baumeisters oder eines Bildhauers oder auch noch das eines Malers, gewiß aber nicht das eines Dichters *oder gar* eines Tonsetzers" (VIII, 84). Risach, who, as he says, has always been strongly drawn toward tangible concrete things ever since his youth ("Die Kräfte...in mir...verlangten Gestalten und bewegten sich um Gestalten" VIII, 82), classifies the arts according to their manifestation of *Gestalten*, "wie sie als *Körper* aus der Bildhauerei und

Baukunst hervorgehen, als *Flächen, Linien* und *Farben* aus der Malerei, als *Folge der Gefühle* in der Musik" (VIII, 82). Whereas Risach indicates that the *Gestalten* of sculpture and architecture are bodies tangibly realized in space, and those of painting are areas, lines, and colors visibly realized on a plane, he does not state analogously that the *Gestalten* of music are the configurations of tones and rhythms acoustically perceptible in time. Instead, he perceives the *Gestalten* of music as a "succession of feelings," a description which, while stretching the concept *Gestalt* beyond its scope, would hardly satisfy such masters of musical form as Bach, Händel, Haydn, or Mozart. Despite the praise Risach gives these classical composers, there is no evidence that he is aware of the tonal and rhythmic structures of their compositions, and one may conclude that with all his admiration for the composers, he does not really understand or appreciate their musical works.

One must deduce from Risach's stress on "feelings" and from his silence on the formal elements in music that he responds to music only on the emotional level and evaluates it purely as emotional expression. It is his failure to appreciate the formal aspect of music that makes it so difficult for him to fit this art medium into a scheme of *Gestalt*, and thereby leads to his awkward definition, which both overextends the term *Gestalt* by applying it to something as amorphous as "feelings" and does music the injustice of ignoring its own inherent and valid *musical Gestalt*. Lacking an understanding of musical form as such, Risach feels basically uncomfortable with this art, because it is to him devoid of any tangible substance. It appears to him at the farthest remove from the art of sculpture, his favorite art form. With no *Gestalten* save those of "feelings," music becomes the polar opposite of the concrete reality of the marble statue. One can say that compared to this work of sculpture, music, as it is defined and presented by the author, is essentially *gestaltlos*.

The suspicion that music is of questionable character, not in conformity with the high aesthetic-ethical demands of *Gestalt*, is also apparent in the absence of musical performances both at the *Asperhof* and at the *Sternenhof*. Although a piano stands in Mathilde's home, no one is ever said to play it. Mathilde and Natalie play the zither, but only when they are alone. By contrast, the ladies at the *Inghof* entertain guests by singing and playing the piano, but they are inferior to Natalie, the peerless heroine, who categorically declines to perform. The close affinity between music and the irrational is emphasized in the flash-back story about young Mathilde, wherein music becomes the very symbol of uncontrollable passion.

Despite the author's obvious distrust of music, musical expression is not altogether taboo in *Der Nachsommer*. Music is represented in the novel not by orchestral, piano, organ, or violin playing, as one might expect if Risach's praise of the classical composers who wrote for such instruments were founded on a true appreciation of their works. It is the zither, rather, that establishes the character of music in *Der Nachsommer*. This instrument, whose very name in German suggests "trembling," is not suited for formal compositions, but seems designed for intimate expressions of joy and sorrow, love and loss, as heard in folk songs and individual improvisations. In choosing this instrument, the author again points up emotion as the essence of this otherwise formless art.

Stifter does not seek to deny music access to the world of the novel. A number of persons occasionally play the zither. Heinrich, well schooled in many areas of study, even acquires considerable skill at playing a zither of his own, and takes pleasure in teaching this instrument to his sister too. The young people enjoy their hours of music together and are not imperiled by the art that for Mathilde was so daimonic. When practiced with discretion — not excessively and not exclusively — the art of music can serve to enhance life. It has its place in the *Rosenhaus* society, just as feeling and emotion are rightly a part of being. Stifter is not concerned with eliminating any elements of beauty from human life, but with incorporating them harmoniously into his *Bildungsideal*.

Most closely bound to the zither is Joseph, the zither player of the mountains. Joseph's identity is vague. Heinrich identifies him first as a "Jägersmann," but then discards this term as inaccurate, since Joseph has really not served adequately as a hunter. He is, as Heinrich later defines him, more a vagabond, "ein Herumstreicher"

(VII, 3), because he wanders about in the mountains seemingly without aim or purpose, and even his clothes are those of a poor tramp: "Sein Anzug war graues Tuch und sehr abgetragen" (VIII, 228). His whereabouts are unpredictable. It seems to Heinrich at first that he is to be found everywhere, but later for long stretches of time he is to be found nowhere, having vanished without a trace, as is shown by the following passages: "er war fort, und so gut, wie verschollen. Kein Mensch wußte etwas von ihm" (VII, 195); "Mein Zitherspiellehrer, der einige Zeit gleichsam verschollen war..." (VII, 263); "Der Jäger...war...fortgegangen. Wohin er sich begeben habe, wußten die Leute selber nicht'" (VII, 318); "Man sagte mir aber, daß...kein Mensch weder in den nähern, noch in den fernern Thälern etwas von ihm gehört habe" (VIII, 19). His reappearances are as sudden and as inexplicable, and Heinrich can only say: "Mein Zitherspiellehrer...war wieder da" (VII, 263).

Not tied to any useful job, not fettered by the bond of marriage, not restricted in his comings and goings by social requirements, indifferent even to his audience (VIII, 228), Joseph is outside the social order and might be seen as a completely liberated individual, "embodying a secret longing of the author."[7] Far from being truly free and autonomous, however, Joseph is totally possessed ("ergriffen und beherrscht" VII, 265) by his instrument: "Es war, als wenn er nichts auf Erden liebte, als seine Zither" (VIII, 227). His evanescent being, bound to nothing in the world except his zither, has little substance and form. His life is completely given over to music, and his being is absorbed by music. His compositions, or rather "airs" (*Weisen*), similarly lack form;[8] without real beginning and end, they are wholly improvised: "Er trug eine ihm eigenthümliche Weise vor, dann hielt er inne, dann spielte er wieder, dann hielt er wieder inne, und so fort. Es waren lauter Weisen, die er selber ersonnen hatte, oder die ihm vielleicht eben in dem Augenblicke in den Sinn gekommen waren" (VIII, 227). Although Joseph plays with power and skill, no elements of musical structure are perceptible to Heinrich, who hears no themes, melodic lines, rhythms, harmonies, transpositions, counterpoint, or other configurations, but is aware only of the emotional quality — "wild und weich" (VIII, 20) —

and the spiritual impact: "er...greift in seine und in die Tiefen anderer Menschen, und zwar in gute" (VII, 265).

The man whose ambiguous social image is summed up in Heinrich's epithet "mein schweifender Jägersmann" (VIII, 20) becomes Heinrich's zither teacher and his friend. Though Joseph's way of life is disorderly, in his devotion to music and his fidelity to his responsive pupil he reveals a purity of soul appreciated by Heinrich, who even permits Joseph to accompany him very high up in the Kargrat "in der Nähe der höchsten Höhen" (VII, 264).

The music that Joseph produces on his zither, though formless, is great. He is the finest player in the mountains ("der fertigste und berühmteste Zitherspieler,...den es im Gebirge gab" VII, 3); he plays better ("bei weitem schöner" VII, 10) than the concert artist in the city. Heinrich has never heard a sweeter tone on an instrument (VII, 3) and considers the playing "außerordentlich" (VIII, 19). When Joseph comes unexpectedly to play at Heinrich's wedding, the audience is spellbound. As at a religious service, no one breaks the hush afterwards with applause: "Alles, was sich in der Nähe befand, lauschte unbeweglich, und nicht einmal ein Zeichen eines Beifalles wurde laut" (VIII, 227). The term "alles" instead of "alle" suggests that not only the people but even the things of animate and inanimate nature are moved with awe.

High on the Kargrat, Heinrich tries to verbalize the sublimity of Joseph's zither music. Finding it exalted beyond everything, including his powers of description, Heinrich resorts to hyperbole, which he places within quotation marks, revealing thereby his sense of inadequacy and embarrassment: "Alles, was ich...gehört hatte, erblaßte zur Unbedeutenheit [*sic*] gegen sein Spiel, von dem ich den Ausdruck 'höchste Herrlichkeit' gebrauchen muß (VII, 264 f.). Heinrich finds that the "glory" of music cannot be encompassed by words or contained in a rational formulation. His descriptive ability fails here, as did Risach's in *his* attempt to formulate the character of music. Joseph, the "hunter" who is not a hunter, is likewise indefinable except in terms of his creative art. Existing solely for his playing and through his playing, his being is so completely fused with his music that he too, like his formless but sublime art, is more spirit than *Gestalt*. In his ambiguity and *Gestaltlosigkeit*, he is the human manifestation of music. Upon the Kargrat it is evident that he is an exalted character, who belongs on the mountains as does the zither: "Sie [the zither] erschien mir als ein Gegenstand, der nur allein in die Berge gehört und mit den Bergen Eins ist" (VI, 35).

Stifter's reticence in presenting the musician and Heinrich's embarrassment in describing music can be explained by their dedication to the *Gestalt* principle. While recognizing the ineffable glory of music, Heinrich is more at ease with the clearly defined forms of painting and sculpture. While elevating music to the highest mountains, the author cannot give full approbation to the musician. In the presentation of Joseph, the author suggests that the integrity of man's *Gestalt* may be imperiled by excessive exposure to the art whose essence for him is *Gestaltlosigkeit*. Nevertheless Stifter gave to his irregular musician a certain charm and to his formless music a certain splendor, thus affirming the mystery of beauty beyond the rational order of perfect *Gestalt*.[9]

VI

THE MONSTROUS PAINTING

Among the many art works described by Heinrich, there is one painting so extraordinary as to merit special attention. This painting, by the artist Roland, can easily be overlooked in the novel, because the author devotes only a scant paragraph to it. The picture demands consideration, however, because there are several signs indicating its significance: Heinrich's father, a knowledgeable collector, pronounces it "höchst bedeutend" (VIII, 203);[1] Heinrich's sagacious mentor Risach offers to finance a travel program for the artist because the painting shows so much talent; Roland himself is euphoric about the painting ("in einer gehobenen, schwebenden Stimmung" VIII, 237), because it proves that he has it in him to create a masterpiece.

The painting is placed in the *Marmorsaal* on the top floor of the *Rosenhaus*, elevated to a hall of high distinction. Despite this honor, the painting never achieves prominence in the novel, but tends to disappear among the many other, more exhaustively described objects. The author's apparent reticence in dealing with this "significant" work presents one of the interesting ambiguities in *Der Nachsommer*. The mystery is heightened for the attentive reader, who observes that the painting is altogether an anomaly in the novel, for the scene it offers clashes provocatively with the ideal world which *Der Nachsommer* projects. One cannot help but be jarred by an art work which seems to flout the principle of *Gestalt* underlying the world of the novel. The following examination of the artist and his disturbing creation will attempt to resolve some ambiguities of the strange painting and relate it to the philosophic basis of the novel.

According to Roland, the picture gives a revelation of his inner self with "Gestaltungen, wie sie sich in dem Gemüthe finden" (VIII, 53). It is then not merely a "landscape," as Heinrich calls it, but an inscape revelatory and expressive of the artist himself. Therefore it is not surprising that the reserve Stifter shows in his presentation of the painting is evidenced also in his treatment of Roland.

Roland's appearances are restricted to a minimum. By contrast with his brother, who is an almost constant presence at the *Asperhof*, where both are employed, Roland receives only brief mention. The brother, Eustach, a skilled craftsman, whose character and interests emulate those of his master Risach, is held in high esteem by all. The problematical character of Roland by contrast causes worry to Risach: "Es hat Schwierigkeiten mit diesem jungen Manne, ich wünsche sein Wohl" (VIII, 234). Within Roland there burns "fire" capable both of flaring up into great art and of threatening the existence of the artist himself (VIII, 234). Roland is less mature and flexible than his brother. Nevertheless, he has one incomparable quality which gives him distinction over Eustach: he has the power ("Kraft" VI, 293) of a real artist.

This power does not always remain within proper bounds, but may break out in violence, as Heinrich points out: "Ich fand in ihm einen sehr feurigen Mann von starken Entschlüssen, und *von heftigem Begehren*" (VII, 5). He has a touch of arrogance or sullenness, as indicated by his "aufgeworfene Lippen" (VI, 247); his tendencies are revolutionary and potentially destructive: "Roland war entschieden für Neuerung, wenn sie auch alles umstürzte" (VII, 247). It is not surprising that the author has mixed feelings about a man who does not live in accord with Stifter's "sanftes Gesetz" but who has nevertheless the power, the fire, and the determination of genius.

The author's attitude toward Roland's painting seems to be similarly ambivalent. Though Risach and Drendorf admire it, Heinrich is much less positive. He avoids saying that he likes the painting, but characterizes it merely as "merkwürdig" (VIII, 52), an ambiguous term, which could be approbatory: "remarkable," or derogatory: "strange, peculiar." It is unlikely that lack of aesthetic assurance would be the reason for Heinrich's use of such a vague term at this stage of his development, for his education in art has already been effected, and on several occasions previously he has expressed sophisticated evaluations of art works. More likely, Heinrich's noncommittal characterization may indicate a certain reservation on his part, or even an attempt to hide an antipathy.

Heinrich first expresses astonishment, if not disapproval, at the size of the canvas, which goes beyond the bounds of what is proper. He points out that it is so huge that it can't even be taken out of the room without being rolled up. Regarding the scene presented on the canvas, Heinrich seems disappointed at the lack of images. Far from seeing any *Gestaltungen,* either of external nature or of the inner psyche, Heinrich perceives rather the *absence* of forms. From his description we hear more of what is not to be seen on the canvas than of what is, and finally the reader is left with nothing to be envisioned except craggy rocks, dry grasses, and rubble, with clouds overhead — an exposure of a desolate wasteland. Heinrich creates the impression of desolation and wilderness for the reader by first naming and then taking away an assortment of landscape images *not* in the picture, and by developing entangled sentences of excessive syntactical complexity:

> (1) Auf diesem wüsten Raume waren *nicht* Berge *oder* Wasserfluthen *oder* Ebenen *oder* Wälder *oder* die glatte See mit schönen Schiffen dargestellt, (2) sondern es waren starre Felsen da, (3) die *nicht* als geordnete Gebilde empor standen, (4) sondern, wie zufällig, als Blöcke und selbst hie und da schief in der Erde staken, gleichsam als Fremdlinge, (5) die, (6) wie jene Normannen, auf dem Boden der Insel, die ihnen *nicht* gehörte, sich seßhaft gemacht hatten. (7) Aber der Boden war *nicht,* wie der jener Insel, (8) oder vielmehr, er war so, (9) wo er *nicht* von den im Alterthume berühmten Kornfeldern bekleidet *oder* von den dunkeln fruchtbringenden Bäumen bedeckt ist, (10) sondern wo er zerrissen und vielgestaltig (11) *ohne* Baum und Strauch (12) mit den dürren Gräsern, (13) den weißleuchtenden Furchen, (14) in denen ein aus unzähligen

Steinen bestehender *Quarz angehäuft ist*, (15) und mit dem *Gerölle* und mit dem *Trümmerwerke*, (16) das überall *ausgesä't ist*, (17) der *dörrenden Sonne entgegen schaut*. (VIII, 52 f.; italics and numbering mine.)

In this desolate scene there are not any of the things of which Heinrich is fond. With a sense of loss he enumerates them. When he evokes the image of the sea, his nostalgia for concrete forms would even supply additionally the "lovely ships" to relieve the emptiness of an imagined seascape without "things" on it.[2] The rocks, "starr" with the rigidity of lifelessness (2), are not formations ("Gebilde") such as orderly, and thus benign, *Gestalten* (3), for there is something haphazard, and wrong, about their presence ("wie zufällig...hie und da schief" 4). They are called not euphoniously "Gebilde," but harshly "Blöcke"; they do not "stand up straight" by themselves, but are merely "stuck" into the ground. They resemble the Normans, strangers in an alien land (6). But since the image of the British Isles is too pleasant to convey the true atmosphere sensed by Heinrich (7), he substitutes for this image a vague and negative reference to antiquity (8, 9), from which, however, all trace of fertility ("den Kornfeldern, fruchtbringenden Bäumen") is removed, and the barren earth is stripped of any covering ("nicht...bekleidet, oder...bedeckt"), which might relieve its stark ugliness. The ground is torn and polymorphic (10); vegetation is lacking ("ohne Baum und Strauch" 11); grasses are mentioned only to heighten the effect of aridity, with the adjective "dürr" (12). Instead of harvested crops heaped in the furrows (14), there are piles of lifeless quartz, white like gravestones. Incongruously, what has been "sown" here, is not seed, but rubble and ruin in sterile, shattered fragments. This wasteland stares up at a withering sun (17).

The syntax of these two sentences conveys the same impression of sinister disorder. The sentence structure is rough and torn like the landscape, full of manifold configurations, but without symmetry or balance or any appreciable form. The rhythm is irregular and uneven; no orderly arrangement of patterns can be established, no smoothness of flow can be felt. The very sounds and rhythmic stresses of the words intensify the agitation that rises gradually to near panic:

After the nostalgic tone sustained through the enumeration (1), a forceful clause (2) exposes the actuality of the view with the thrice-occurring open "ah." Its third and most emphatic occurrence in "da" is unembellished and declamatory, as if announcing that the wishdreams of (1) are past and the real sight is now being shown. In (4) the tempo accelerates, rushing toward the stressed "Fremdlinge," which permits no pause but leads into a relative clause. The sentence hurtles on through broken up elements to its end. No stop can be made here either, however, because of the coordinating conjunction which begins the next sentence. After the negative (7), Heinrich attempts a positive statement (8), but falters and turns it too into a negative (9), which offers a poetic lament for absent life and beauty. The positive statement that we expect after "sondern" turns out to be a negative image of the earth's laceration and upheaval ("zerrissen und vielgestaltig"). Denying the presence of tree and bush, Heinrich, in a clipped formula: "ohne Baum und Strauch (11), also denies us the softening effect of modifiers to the two monosyllabic nouns, that, like a cry of pain, sound the "au" diphthong. The repeated guttural "r" in "dürren Gräsern" (12), combined with the distasteful long "ä" suggests nausea and the throat-rattle of death, while the unnatural gleam of the furrows, and the word "Furchen" itself, by its similarity to the word "Furcht" (fear), intensify one's malaise. The heaps of countless rocks are presented heavily in highly stressed irregular rhythm: "in denen ein aus unzähligen Steinen bestehender Quarz angehäuft ist." The quickened pace, felt already in the preceding sentence, drives on relentlessly without any restful pause, through a number of fragmentary phrases and their appendages. After yet another harsh element: "Gerölle und Trümmerwerke" (with 4 gutturals) and another modifying clause, we reach the concluding verb of the clause begun in (10), and come to a final halt (17).

Throughout this description we do not so much see a landscape as experience a nightmarish wasteland, where men, the "strangers" symbolized by rocks, are haphazardly thrown into an alien and unregulated world, and mankind, through the viewer Heinrich, is confronted with death, sterility, and meaninglessness. The disrupted and precipitate style of the two sentences betrays Heinrich's mounting anguish, as he vainly tries to recall the beneficence of the absent forms. His increasing anxiety and existential awareness of a reality devoid of forms and beauty can be traced through the tortuous syntax and jagged rhythm, and can be sensed in the profuse anti-images. In the end, bereft of cherished illusions, Heinrich faces an earth without the grace of *Gestalten* and is exposed to the hostility of the universe, as embodied by the withering sun.

It is clear from Heinrich's tortuous description that he is facing an extreme situation, for in Stifter's smooth prose even a ripple indicates a disturbance. While it is generally true, as Lunding claims, that Stifter tries to shield his characters from the threats and mysteries of the void,[3] existential terror is not unknown to the characters of *Der Nachsommer*. Such moments are signaled by the rare harsh sounds, rough passages, and images of unpleasant association that suddenly break into the serenely flowing prose and briefly cloud the golden glow of the novel's atmosphere. One may say, however, that Stifter does not leave his characters suspended in fright and anguish, at least not in this novel, but he provides them with the ability to overcome the threat to their selfhoood.

While Heinrich's tone becomes strident, it does not reach hysteria, and while the syntax approaches incoherence, it never wholly disintegrates. Heinrich does not break down in this critical confrontation with the vision of an irrational universe; he does not surrender to despair. Fixing his gaze on the canvas, he is gradually able to see in this "wüsten Raum" some elements of spatial composition, and in the torrid sky a kind of beauty, after all. His will to live asserts itself as a will to form.

Like a great gong, the word "so" tolls thrice, announcing a transformation of the vision. Three clauses of increasing length and deliberation depict the three stages in the reestablishment of Heinrich's equilibrium:

(1) So war Rolands Boden,

(2) so bedeckte er die ungeheure Fläche,
(3) und so war er in sehr großen und einfachen Abtheilungen gehalten,...

First, in a simple statement of fact Heinrich accepts the representation as reality to be faced dispassionately. Second, he recognizes that even this harsh and forbidding landscape is a kind of blessing by "covering up" a greater monstrosity, that of the otherwise vast emptiness of the canvas (much as man's image-making, in art and religion, conceals the otherwise annihilating monstrosity of the infinite space of the universe). Third and finally, Heinrich becomes aware that the painting has some organization into large, plain areas.

The rhythm of these clauses also demonstrates Heinrich's gradual recovery:

(1) Sō war Rōlands Bōden,
(2) sō bedeckte er die ūngeheure Flāche,
(3) ūnd sō war er in sehr grōßen und einfāchen Abtheilūngen gehalten,...

The heavy spondees in (1) suggest the weight of Heinrich's realization and the burden of his acceptance, a burden which gradually eases, however, as shown by the lighter trochees toward the end of the clause. The regular trochees moving without a break through (2) provide an objective pattern that makes no creative demands upon Heinrich. Finally (3) with its rhythmic variation and unimpeded flow reveals that Heinrich has recovered from shock and has regained freedom of expression. The form of these clauses reinforces the meaning of the statement itself: By sheer determination Heinrich has imposed order on apparent chaos and thereby restored his own serenity.

The second half of the sentence, also comprising three clauses, has the following structure:

(1) und über ihm *w*aren Wolken,
(2) *w*elche

     (a) einzeln und vielzählig,
     (b) *sch*immernd und *Sch*atten *w*erfend
     (c) in einem Himmel *s*tanden,
 (3) *w*elcher
     (a) tief
     (b) und heiß
     (c) und südlich *w*ar

 (1) continues in the calm tone of the preceding part of the sentence. The "w" of "waren Wolken" introduces the alliteration that is repeated in the introductory words of (2) and (3) and thereby relates the clauses. Sounded again in the final word "war" (3c) with its staticity of concept it produces an effect of unchanging and infinite duration. The threefold description of clouds (2a, b, c) presents the aesthetic play of light and shadow, introducing with the alliterative "schimmernd, Schatten, standen" a further quieting device. With mention of "Himmel" (2c) and its threefold attributes (3a, b, c) it becomes clear that Heinrich's contemplation, previously focused on the "dörrende Sonne," has expanded to a realm beyond fear — "tief" and "heiß" suggest profundity and intensity, but not destructiveness. The adjective "südlich" evokes the atmosphere of antiquity, positively, at last, as the matrix of beauty. After the rhythmic and descriptive embellishments and the rapt tone of (2), there follows in (3) a retardation, a focus on essentials, and an increasing quietude, culminating in the deep, restful tone of the cadence.

 Heinrich never gives an evaluation of the painting, which is for him a personal experience that challenges his being and his faith. At first plunged into confusion by the revelation of the chaotic void, he neither denies its reality nor does he accept it as ultimately valid. As he looks unflinching at the canvas, the very chaos begins to take shape. He sees clouds shimmering, and these again create kindly shadows, which provide a shield from the sun. His determination to find meaning in the universe manifests itself as ability to visualize *Gestalten*, to create, if necessary, by his own will, the redemptive *Gestalt*.

 As Heinrich's turmoil was illustrated in the convulsed syntax of the first sentence describing the painting, so his creative ability is reflected in the masterful composition of this sentence, which, laid out in its structural elements, reveals a *Gestalt* of pleasing balance and proportion:

I
(1) So war Rolands Boden,
(2) so bedeckte er die ungeheure Fläche,
(3) und so war er in sehr großen und einfachen Abtheilungen gehalten,

II
(1) und über ihm waren Wolken
(2) welche
    (a) einzeln und vielzählig,
    (b) schimmernd und Schatten werfend
    (c) in einem Himmel standen,
(3) welcher
    (a) tief
    (b) und heiß
    (c) und südlich war.

Heinrich's discomposure at viewing the formlessness of the painting indicates that *Gestaltlosigkeit* is a threat to man's integrity. Chaos is potentially destructive, and it is for this reason that the author exercises such restraint in presenting Roland's painting to the reader. The author's concern is for integrated *Gestalt*, in man's works and in man himself. Like Heinrich, who reacts to the painting with distress until he is able to see, even here, the concrete forms he requires, so the author is uneasy about the inner chaos of Roland and requires that this genius undergo the formative influence of travel and study, which, presumably, will mold him into a more acceptable *Gestalt*.

Despite its questionable aspect, formlessness had a certain fascination for the author, who accepts Roland and his painting, with reservations, as he accepts Joseph and his music. The strange painting, devoid of forms, has a mysterious beauty incommensurable with that of the *Marmorgestalt*, which stands as the measure of perfection in the novel. In placing the painting in the *Marmorsaal*, which is situated higher than the hallway where the *Marmorgestalt* stands, the author acknowledges *Gestaltlosigkeit* as a basic and universal concept, which can be regarded as a complement to the principle of *Gestalt* or even as a challenge to its supremacy.[4]

VII

THE EQUIVOCAL LIGHT OF THE
MARMORSAAL: TRACES OF MYSTICISM

In the well-ordered *Rosenhaus* there is one room unlike all the others. The *Marmorsaal*, on the top floor, up beyond the magnificent marble sculpture of the Greek maiden, has about it an aura of mystery, because it alone, of all the rooms in Risach's home, seems to have no content, no utility, and no purpose. In this novel, where functionalism is programmatic, a room empty and useless presents a baffling anomaly, which demands clarification. This study proposes to examine and interpret the strange nature of the *Marmorsaal* and to establish what its presence in the novel might signify.

To be sure, Heinrich does ascribe to the *Marmorsaal* a function: "Er war eine Sammlung von Marmor" (VI, 88).[1] If the *Marmorsaal* were intended to be intrinsically an exhibition hall, it would be an unusual and peculiar one, for it does not contain any pieces of marble other than those of which it is made, and even these pieces are not labeled to give information about the varieties represented. When Heinrich enters the room for the first time, he supplies no mineralogical data for the reader, but notes only that the delicate colors of the marble walls are aesthetically combined and the bright hues of the floor pieces are smoothly joined to form "a lovely picture" ("der Fußboden, wie ein liebliches Bild" VI, 88).

When Heinrich tells his host, Risach, who is giving him a guided tour of the estate, how much he likes the arrangement, Risach looks pleased, but doesn't comment. Heinrich makes special mention of this reticence: "er sprach aber nicht weiter darüber" (VI, 89). Since Risach has been most obliging to explain the many interesting features of his house in great detail, his silence here seems odd. Heinrich finds another feature of the hall so remarkable that he emphasizes it with three negatives: "In dem Saale war kein Bild, kein Stuhl, kein Geräthe" (VI, 88). There is nothing in the room; there are not even flowers, such as are present everywhere else: "in allen Zimmern *mit Ausnahme des Marmorsaales* an jedem nur einiger Maßen geeigneten Platze [hatte ich] Blumen aufgestellt gesehen" (VI, 94).

Before entering the *Marmorsaal*, or ascending the stairs up to it, one must remove one's shoes and put on soft-soled slippers. While Heinrich regards this regulation as a sensible measure to avoid marring the beautiful and delicate flooring, the attention which the author gives to this practice seems excessive: whenever Risach or Heinrich are walking in this hall, they are said to be treading softly in their slippers; with every mention of the hall, there is reference to shoe removal. We wonder whether such emphasis on what seems, after all, merely a practical expedient, is just an instance of Stifter's reputed prolixity,[2] or whether the author is using the device of irritating repetition to draw our attention more sharply to the *Marmorsaal*. If the author is giving us a sign — and by now most scholars agree that Stifter writes more with purpose than pedantry — then his insistence upon shoe removal must signalize that this is no ordinary room for the mere display of marble, but a very special hall, worthy of precautionary measures and worthy of notice.

While the repeated mention of shoe removal must indicate the noteworthy character of the hall, the act itself, observed in some religions as a ritual preliminary to entering a holy place, may here also have ritualistic connotation. The familiar Biblical legend of Moses and the burning bush is an instance of the use of this motif within the Judeo-Christian tradition. Stifter, who probably knew the story already as a child, certainly read it in the Benedictine monastery school of Kremsmünster, where study of the Bible was part of basic curriculum. Of all Old Testament stories, this dramatic encounter of Moses and the Lord must have made a strong impression upon the young Stifter, for God's command: "Zieh deine Schuhe von deinen Füßen ab; denn der Ort, worauf du stehest, ist ein heiliges Land," (Moses II, 3, 5, as quoted from a translation by Jos. Bern.

Benedict Venusi, in the edition of Prag, 1820, which was in use at Kremsmünster while Stifter was there in residence) still seems to resonate in Risach's admonition to Heinrich.

The regulation of wearing slippers in certain areas of the *Rosenhaus* can, of course, be explained on purely practical grounds. It is indeed characteristic of *Der Nachsommer* that everything takes place and has meaning initially on the realistic plane. It is this distinctive feature that led to many of the negative commentaries by early critics, who found the novel dull and long-winded. On the surface of the novel very little happens, and there seems to be, on this level, unnecessary repetition and excessive attention to detail. But when the work is read with attention to its overtones, undercurrents, and symbolism, the depths are challenging and fathomless. Far from being a tedious work, *Der Nachsommer* is then rather a cryptic masterpiece full of ciphers, the "things" that yield their messages only to patient probing of the details of their presentation. The *Marmorsaal* is one such hieroglyph.

While the many things of *Der Nachsommer* express the author's ideology through their *Gestalt*, the marble hall is *gestaltlos*, is empty and silent. Its meaning cannot be deduced from qualities of form and material. Containing no *Gestalt*, it lacks philosophic theory; its message is ineffable. As Heinrich ascends beyond the graspable reality of the marble statue, he enters a realm filled only with the glow of marble and the fragrance of roses: "Zu dem Glanze des Marmors war der Saal auch mit Rosenduft erfüllt" (VI, 88). Such intangibles however, not only do fill its emptiness, but even *fulfill* it, as the term "erfüllt" (instead of the more common "gefüllt") indicates. Since marble is symbolic of the love between Heinrich and Natalie, and roses are symbolic of the love between Risach and Mathilde,[3] the *glow* of marble and the *fragrance* of roses may be regarded as the distilled essence of these affections. As candle-light and incense fill a chapel, glow of marble and fragrance of rose fill the *Marmorsaal*, fulfilling it with their spiritual substance. Whether thought of as Eros or Agape, love is by tradition the human emotion of distinctly divine origin. Shared by man and God, love is a medium between the two, a bridge whereby mankind and Deity can reach

each other. The presence of love, suggested by the glow and fragrance in the *Marmorsaal*, can be said to "fulfill" it if the *Marmorsaal* is seen as a hall with a spiritual purpose: it is to be a realm of communion between God and man.

Consideration of a similar hall at the *Sternenhof* will strengthen the conjecture that the purpose of the *Marmorsaal* is a religious one. The marble floor in the *Sternenhof* hall is likewise highly polished to mirror all things, and it was designed, says Risach, according to a sketch of church windows. The religious note introduced by this ecclesiastical reference is reinforced by Heinrich's sensation of being seized by a feeling of awe: "Es ergriff Einen ein Gefühl eines Bedeutungsvollen." He describes the floor in superlative terms of emotional quality: "Es war der *ernsteste* und *feurigste* Teppich." With all its serious and inspirational character, however, the hall at the *Sternenhof* does not fully lose secular character, for within it there are still pieces of furniture, albeit only those of finest quality: "die schönsten und wohlerhaltensten alten Schreine und andere Einrichtungsstücke" (VI, 324). While claiming a spiritual dimension, the hall at the *Sternenhof* does not pretend to the uncompromising austerity of the empty *Marmorsaal* high in the *Rosenhaus*.

No ordinary activities are carried on in the *Marmorsaal*: one does not work here — there are no instruments of work; one does not rest here — there is not even a chair. One can stand and look at the marble inside and the spectacle of nature outside. One can pace back and forth, as Risach does during a storm. One can converse. It is here that some of the most important discourses on aesthetics, philosophy, and religion are held. When Heinrich enters the hall, just after he has had the thrilling revelation of the *Marmorgestalt*, he proceeds immediately to inquire about that statue: "Warum habt Ihr mir denn nicht gesagt, ...daß die Bildsäule...so schön ist?" (VII, 75) whereupon Risach reveals to him the whole history of the sculpture since he first saw it. His long recital about the acquisition and restoration of this art work leads him to general observations about Greek art and medieval art. Then he considers expression through art itself, and takes up the concept of mimesis, the principle of "movement in repose," the nature and the effect of beauty — a discourse which finally leads to a religious conclusion, namely that man endeavors through art to imitate God, the greatest and the only true artist ("den größten und einzigen Künstler... Gott" VII, 95).

After this discourse, replete with wisdom and rational theories, the action of the two men takes them beyond the realm of reason. They step to the window and observe a storm, an apparition of indescribable and increasing grandeur: "Wir betrachteten eine Weile die Erscheinung vor uns, die über dem immer dunkler werdenden Gefilde immer großartiger wurde" (VII, 95).

A comparison between Heinrich's impression of the hall on this occasion and his previous purely factual report shows that he has gained an awareness of the extraordinary nature of the *Marmorsaal*. His appreciation now goes beyond recognition of the lovely colors and of the skilled workmanship evident in the arrangement. The revelation of the beauty of the Greek statue seems to have made him receptive to the spiritual aspect of the hall, for now he speaks of the "seriousness" of its isolation and grandeur: "Zu dem Ernste der Wolkenwände gesellt sich der Ernst der Wände von Marmor, und daß in dem Saale gar keine Geräthe sind, vermehrt noch die Einsamkeit und Größe" (VII, 87). The repetition of the word "Ernst" stresses the awesomeness of the hall, which, clear of impeding profane objects, unites the solemnity of the clouds outside with the solemnity of the marble within.

According to Risach, the hall is not for habitation, but for beholding: "eigentlich nicht zum Bewohnen, sondern nur zum Besehen bestimmt" (VI, 96). What is to be seen here is translucent marble inside and a wide expanse of earth and sky outside. Heinrich's depiction of the view stresses its "wholeness" and the reciprocity between the vision and the beholder. An abundance of the heavens "looks in"; a whole chain of the Alps can be seen: "Durch die hellen Fenster schaut *der ganze* südliche Himmel herein, und auch Theile des westlichen und des östlichen sind zu erblicken. Die *ganze* Kette der hiesigen Alpen kann am Rande des Gesichtskreises gesehen werden" (VII, 87). Risach seeks out the hall during thunderstorms to observe the majestic display of the storm spread out below.

As the two men pace back and forth, the lightning flashes and is reflected beneath them and around them on the mirror surfaces of the marble ("Spiegelflächen um und unter uns" VII, 90). The marble, previously said to reflect the "Ernst" of the clouds, here is said to reflect the flashes of light. Separation between the outer and the inner disappears as all is unified in a pervasive glow: "einige Male [war] der reine, kalte Marmor, wie in eine Glut, getaucht, und nur die hölzernen Thüren standen dunkel in dem Feuer" (VII, 87). Heinrich's beholding reaches an intensity that recalls Moses' vision, as the marble turns incandescent and the dark wooden doors seem to stand in a fire. The light imagery suggests the burning bush, the vision of God.

When interpreted in terms of mystical tradition, the outside light streaming in represents the Divine Spirit flowing into a human soul, which must be empty and isolated like the *Marmorsaal*. The "reine, kalte Marmor," infused with glow, images the pure, dispassionate condition of a soul reflecting the Divine Light. Vibrant with the light radiating between Source and mirror, the *Marmorsaal* is an image of mystical union, wherein separation between outside and inside, human and Divine, no longer exists.[4]

Traces of mysticism can be found throughout the novel. The phenomenon most directly inviting comparison with the *Marmorsaal* is the starry sky, where intense light and absence of form are likewise the elements through which Heinrich apprehends a reality beyond his comprehension. Although in this novel of *Gestalten* it might be expected that Heinrich would take an interest in the constellations, as the *Gestalten* of the sky, this is not the case. While the clouds and the moon are still felt to be forms, all that is beyond them, space and stars, belong to the realm of vast infinity, bewildering to man. Early in the novel Heinrich's descriptions of the night sky express negative feelings as, for example, the paragraph (with eight negations), which describes Heinrich's state of mind on the evening of Natalie's first arrival at the *Rosenhaus*: "Ich war sehr traurig.... Es standen nicht die Wolken am Himmel, die ihn nach Richtungen durchzogen und ihm Gestaltung gaben, sondern es *brannte* bereits über dem ganzen Gewölbe der einfache und ruhige

Sternenhimmel" (VI, 276). Heinrich's melancholy is deepened by the lack of clouds which, if present, would give some form to the sky. He also is distressed by the apparent unconcern of the "einfache und ruhige Sternenhimmel" whose serene burning suggests a cosmic power indifferent to man.

On a later occasion he expresses frustration at his inability to distinguish the countless stars, and he voices his nostalgia for a distinct form of light, such as the moon, or even just a tiny bit of moon: "Weiter war nichts zu unterscheiden als der glänzende Himmel, ... der von unzähligen Sternen, aber *nicht von dem geringsten Stückchen* Mond beleuchtet war" (VI, 317). Only much later, after he has acquired aesthetic insight and emotional maturity, does he overcome his antipathy to the formlessness of the sky and affirm its splendor: "Es stand kein Mond in demselben [Nachthimmel] und keine Wolke, aber in der milden Nacht brannten so viele Sterne, als wäre der Himmel mit ihnen angefüllt, und als berührten sie sich gleichsam mit ihren Spitzen. Die Feierlichkeit traf mich erhebender, und die Pracht des Himmels war mir eindringender, als sonst" (VII, 297).

In contemplating the starry sky, Heinrich senses a grandeur which he speaks of both in the singular ("die verschwundene stille Größe" VII, 298) and in the plural ("zu jenen Größen,...von denen wir eine Ahnung haben" VII, 297), because infinite greatness can be as little defined by number as by form. He responds to the infinitude of the starry sky with worship: "Es war eine Weihe und Verehrung des Unendlichen in mir" (VII, 298). He even asks himself whether the formless glory of the star-filled night is not greater than the clarity of day, which brings out all the forms: "Haben da meine vom Nachtwachen brennenden Augen die verschwundene stille Größe nicht für höher erkannt, als den klaren Tag, der alles deutlich macht?" (VII, 298).

Strengthened by the knowledge of man's innate godliness as revealed through the marble statue, and ennobled by Natalie's love, he can endure a starry sky devoid of moon and clouds and exult in the majesty of infinite light.[5] His terminology is that of mystical tradition: the light strikes and lifts him ("Die Feierlichkeit traf mich erhebender") and glory penetrates him ("die Pracht des Himmels war mir eindringender"). The shift in Heinrich's attitude from dismay to exaltation at the challenge of a reality beyond the formations of earth implies that man can bear the vision of infinity when he has attained his own full stature.

The idea presented through the gradual change in Heinrich's attitude toward the starry sky is expressed more succinctly in a late passage pertaining to the *Marmorsaal*. Here too Heinrich has an experience hard to bear which can be communicated only by the use of light imagery: "Ich ging... in den Marmorsaal. Seine Größe, seine Leerheit, der, wenn ein solches Wort erlaubt ist, dunkle Glanz, der von dem dunkeln und mit ungewissen und zweideutigen Lichtern wechselnden Tage auf seinen Wänden lag und wechselte, ließ sich *nach dem Anblicke der Gestalt des Alterthums tragen und ertragen*" (VIII, 63).

In expressing his sense of the vast void of the hall, Heinrich adds another descriptive term which he assigns to the third and emphatic position of the series: "Seine Größe, seine Leerheit, der... *dunkle Glanz*." Besides noting the emphasis upon this concept, we should note that Heinrich uses it almost apologetically ("wenn ein solches Wort erlaubt ist"). His hesitation before such an antithetical combination shows that he regards it as a formulation not strictly rational, and therefore not strictly proper. The fact that he nevertheless uses it indicates that only such a paradoxical term could render his impression of the strange luminosity reflected on the walls by the day outside, which alternates between dimness and indefinite, equivocal lights ("dem dunkeln und mit ungewissen und zweideutigen Lichtern wechselnden Tage").

The great empty hall, darkly glowing with flickering light, is a realm for which the revelation of the *Marmorgestalt* has readied him. Having seen the noble form, he can "bear" the ambiguous space of the marble hall. Contemplation of the *Gestalt* is like a spiritual exercise preparing Heinrich to enter the greatness of the *Nihil* and "endure" the darkness of the Light.

It has been stated repeatedly by scholars that Stifter has no mystical inclination, but worships the Divine only as it is visibly immanent in the world,[6] and there is indeed much evidence, especially in *Der Nachsommer*, that Stifter is in principle devoted to the things of this world as revelations of immanent Deity. Kurt Michel, however, exaggerates Stifter's this-worldliness in declaring that, for the author, the world and its things provide the only access to God, and that mysticism, in terms of Christian revelation, is utterly alien to him.[7] One should hesitate to claim, as Michel does, that Stifter had no existential conception of the supernatural grace which climaxes in the beatific vision.[8] Surely the wonderful vision in *Bergkristall*, for example, radiates supernatural grace, as Michael Böhler has observed: "In dieser begnadeten Erzählung gelingt das Wunder: die Epiphanie des Göttlichen in Herrlichkeit und Lichterglanz."[9] As in this early work, so there are also moments in *Der Nachsommer* when the Holy Spirit is perceived unmediated and transcendent, notably in the presence of the infinite light of the starry sky and in the equivocal light of the *Marmorsaal*.

To be sure, the author's focus in *Der Nachsommer* is mainly upon the *Gestalten*. Throughout the novel Heinrich learns how wonderful are all the *Gestalten* of nature, art, and humanity when ideally presented. However, the concept "Gestalt" also has religious connotations here, and signifies more than classic perfection of form, for it gives evidence of the union between spirit and matter, between God and the world.[10]

The author states through his spokesman Risach that the *Gestalten* are predicated upon God who is both their Creator and their essence: "Gott, der so unzählige Gestaltungen erschaffen hat" (VII, 95); "Gott...gab uns...Theile des Göttlichen in verschiedenen Gestalten" (VII, 356).

Der Nachsommer is basically a religious work written in praise of the things of earth as manifestations of God. In considering the *Gestalt* as the basic element of the theology underlying *Der Nachsommer*, it would be a mistake to neglect the traces of mysticism that emerge occasionally in the novel and become especially pronounced in the descriptions of the *Marmorsaal*, which is situated higher than the Greek statue, and contains no forms.[11] The hall does contain a Presence, almost overwhelming to Heinrich, indescribable, but sensed through reflected flashes of lightning. Mystical perceptions are not lacking but are transmuted into restrained artistic imagery in this novel, where they add strange illumination to what would otherwise be an almost too brightly enlightened view of the world.

The author is consistently reticent about discussing matters of religion. The foregoing analysis, while pointing out imagery parallel to that of mysticism in literary tradition, attempts neither sharp definition of the term, nor specific proof of Heinrich's mystical experiences. One cannot be explicit about the awesome *Marmorsaal*, because the experience it suggests is by definition ineffable, like the Infinite Spirit, which can be neither presented nor grasped, as the author reminds us: "wer hat erst die Unendlichkeit des Geistes darzustellen gewußt, die schon in der Endlichkeit einzelner Dinge liegt... Oder wer hat nur diesen Geist zu fassen gewußt?" (VII, 152).[12]

VIII

THE HUMAN *GESTALTEN* AND THE FOOLS

The aesthetic-ethical unity which informs the characters in the foreground and establishes them as *Gestalten* in the ideal sense of the term is conspicuously absent from a few peripheral figures. While the human *Gestalten* enjoy both significance in the novel and felicity within their world, the secondary characters who do not measure up to the author's standards are denied both prominence and fulfillment. Since they appear but briefly and have little effect on the plot or Heinrich Drendorf's development, their presence would seem redundant and their introduction into this austere work a puzzling caprice on the part of the author, were it not for their correlation with the main concept which integrates all of its elements. The second-rate, inferior characters still in their negative way serve the author's convictions. Negative and contrasting figures, they may be considered non-*Gestalten,* or in some instances, anti-*Gestalten*. Altogether, they function as cacophonous embellishments enhancing the theme of *Gestalt* which resounds through this novel.

Ostensibly so trivial that they can easily be dismissed as meaningless oddities, these minor figures have not yet been investigated by scholars understandably more interested in the main characters, who not only carry the action but encompass the author's values, as Wolfgang Paulsen has noted: "Die Menschen Stifters gewinnen in immer steigendem Maße die Funktion Schalen zu sein, Schalen für überpersönliche — nicht aber un-persönliche — Inhalte."[1] Horst Glaser has noticed "die peripheren Personen," but he mentions only the *Zitherspiellehrer,* the *Bergführer, Wirtinnen,* and *Landarbeiter,* all of whom, he says, are deprived of individuality, "So verschwinden sie in den Dingen."[2] According to Glaser, the peripheral characters represent only the poorer classes, whom the author relegated to unobtrusive position because attention to them would threaten the credibility of the idyll he constructed.[3]

Actually, however, there is no class distinction between the main and peripheral characters as such. The prominent characters in *Der Nachsommer* are all ideal, but they are not all of the wealthy class; among the peripheral characters there are both ideal and nonideal figures, and they belong to various classes. As an argument against Glaser's accusation, it must be pointed out that among the peripheral characters the moneyed class is represented by figures relatively unattractive, while the working class is represented by figures who more nearly approximate the ideal, such as the gardener, the craftsmen, the servants, and even the rather indigent zither-teacher. In *Der Nachsommer* money and worldly status are not, in themselves, criteria of worth, nor is lack of these possessions a mark of inferiority. Neither is social class the factor which determines the prominence of the characters within the novel.

The criterion of worth in *Der Nachsommer* is the attainment of *Gestalt*. The main characters all have the qualities of *Gestalten*; the peripheral characters are diverse: some are *Gestalten* and some are fools. For all characters, social class is merely an incidental factor. It is Stifter's *Humanitätsideal* — more precisely, his ideal of *Gestalt* — which distinguishes the good from the bad, separates the human *Gestalten* from the fools, as the following study will show.

In *Der Nachsommer* the German *Bildungsroman* reaches the acme of its development: "Der 'Nachsommer' ist der Bildungsroman schlechthin, ein rührend-unheimlich deutsches Buch aus Österreich, welches dem Leser das Menschlichwerden zeigen will."[4] Not only does the hero aspire to the *Humanitätsideal* espoused by Goethe, but he is surrounded by myriad objects which also move toward realization of themselves. Beauty and goodness are inextricably bound together in Stifter's art, as Herman Kunisch has observed: "Stifter hat immer wieder betont, daß die Kunst es mit dem Schönen zu tun habe. Diesem *Schönen*, das sich als *Sittliches* in den Dingen sinnlich bekundet und als angenehm empfunden wird...."[5]

The ideal of the good-beautiful, as it was developed in the eighteenth century by classical German authors, who were inspired by the beautiful forms of Greek antiquity and influenced by the ethics of Christianity, is monumentalized in *Der Nachsommer*, where the concept Καλοκαγαθια underlies the concept *Gestalt*. Not only does man need to realize his own highest potential as a good and beautiful *Gestalt*, but he is charged with assisting all the things around him to reach their own fulfillment, as Joachim Müller has noted: "Der Mensch erfüllt sich nur, wenn er, sicher in sich selbst ruhend, die Wirklichkeit gestaltet...."[6] In this role he carries on a function with religious-mystical significance, as Michael Böhler suggests: "Auch ein so eminent klassischer Begriff wie derjenige der Gestalt erfährt also bei Stifter seine Umdeutung ins Religiöse, und alles Gestaltete hat die Aufgabe, ein Zeugnis der Verbindung von Geist und Stoff, von Gott und Welt zu sein."[7]

Of Natalie Killy says, "Sie verkörpert, was auch ihr Verlobter als Jüngling auf dem Wege zum Manne darstellt: die Idee einer bürgerlichen Kalokagathie in einem Zeitalter, das sie, leider, längst überholt hatte."[8] While Natalie is the image of perfect *being*, Risach is the image of perfect *doing*, for his life is totally devoted to service. Emphasizing the two different aspects of the ideal person, Natalie and Risach are complementary figures. One is not less than the other, but each is perfect; together they exemplify the human *Gestalt* in full dimension.

Other persons in the novel are likewise linked to each other by being two representatives of the same type, two aspects of the same concept, as Eric Blackall notes: "Heinrich is simply a Risach in development and Natalie stands in the same relation to Mathilde. Hence the strange unity of this book, which is a prose-poem, lyrical in its one-sidedness and of singular intensity — the expression of one single great thought, a man's vision of the ideal life."[9] The unity is achieved, according to Dorothea Sieber, because all the human figures express the author's own ethical spirit: "Von den unendlich vielen Gestalten des bunten Lebens ging nur eine einzige in seinen Roman ein: seine eigene innere Gestalt, sein eigenes inneres Gesetz, sein sittlicher Wille zur schönen Seele."[10]

The recurrence of the same human types is, according to Hilde

Cohn, a manifestation of the symbolical nature of Stifter's works.[11] The classicistic rigidity of the human beings, as noted by Killy ("die Menschen in einer klassizistischen Starre," p. 97), and the resemblance among the people, especially the women, as mentioned by Glaser ("Stifters Frauengestalten [sind] zum Verwechseln ähnlich," p. 48), give further evidence that Stifter does not portray unique personalities but Platonic ideas. Paul Hankamer formulates the significance and function of the work's *Gestalten* thus: "Sie sind nicht um ihrer einmaligen Persönlichkeit willen bedeutsam, sondern als typische Urbilder in der reinen Menschenwelt, die das Dasein konkret vertreten, indem sie nach ihrer Art der Ordnung gemäß leben."[12] With the term "Urbilder" we are in the realm of myth, and it is perhaps as myth — eternally recurrent, rigidly changeless, beyond life and beyond time — that we can best approach the *Gestalten* of *Der Nachsommer*, who convey the spiritual and eternal quality of the novel itself; as Killy says, "Am sichtbarsten wird die Unstofflichkeit bei der Behandlung der Menschen, deren Hauptfiguren sämtlich auf die Figuration des Dauernden angelegt sind."[13]

Heinrich Drendorf progresses from innocence and potential to sophistication and realization without ever falling into serious error, because he is "ein hoher, sittlich reiner Mensch."[14] Although Heinrich's *Bildungsweg* is arduous, because of a certain ineptitude and awkwardness within his personality — he describes himself as "unbeholfen gegen das Leben" (VII, 41)[15] — and because of the universal existential problems that assail him, he is never threatened by evil from within or without.

Heinrich's friends all exhibit *Humanität* and should be considered members of a true aristocracy, regardless of their possession or lack of a title. Dorothea Sieber notes that, in *Der Nachsommer*, titles may or may not coincide with true nobility: "Wird...der Adel als eine Auszeichnung innerhalb der Gesellschaft anerkannt, ...so gilt der Adel doch nur insofern, als er mit Menschenadel zusammenfällt."[16] While Stifter's ideal of society is an aristocracy, it must be understood as an aristocracy of spirit, not identifiable with the titled class but accessible to members of any class.

Those slight imperfections that still adhere to the élite in *Der*

Nachsommer are in process of being overcome, often through the help of companions. Heinrich's father, for example, does have the tendency to become too engrossed in his business, but Mrs. Drendorf steers him successfully into other, recreational activities. She also guides Klotilde, Heinrich's sister, smoothly through a painful emotional adjustment to Heinrich's engagement. Roland, the master artist, has a problematical spark of genius and a temperament which he must learn to control, but Risach helps him channel his enthusiasm properly. The others — Eustach the craftsman, Simon the gardener, Kasper the mountain-guide, Joseph the musician, the princess in the city, and Heinrich's jeweler friend — are all models of devotion to their task in life. They express the purity of character which derives from single-minded interest in a vocation.

Only on the periphery of the *Nachsommer*-world do we catch a glimpse of defective characters who do not participate fully in the effort to bring about a better world. In failing to carry out man's fundamental task, they also fail to establish themselves as *Gestalten*. Those who wreak destruction upon the things which fate has entrusted to them must be considered villains; those who allow themselves and the things around them to deteriorate must be considered, at the least, fools. Both are reprehensible. In the sober tone of the narrative, the presence of the fools is a bizarre note that reinforces the message of the novel, not directly and positively, but negatively, by contrast.

The actual villains mentioned in the novel are totally barred from the *Nachsommer* realm itself, by distance in time or space. Anonymously presented, they are devoid of a name as they are devoid of human merit.[17] Unworthy of identification are those barbarians of the past who abused the priceless *Marmorgestalt* by encasing its figure in plaster and setting it in a cheap amusement park, and those brutes who allowed irreplaceable monuments of Medieval and Renaissance religious art to be ravaged by time. Unnamed is the soldier of long ago who was so coarse as to wrap his dirty linen in a piece of canvas on which was painted a magnificent Madonna and Child. The callousness of these people insensitive to art can be equated with the depravity of the unknown hunters who kill a beautiful white stag, unfeelingly, merely for sport. Heinrich condemns such hunters as "Mörder" (VI, 33), as Risach rebukes those who take pleasure in killing birds "um einer Lust und Laune willen" (VI, 173). Risach spends his life combating the evil that results from crimes against beauty and life — by rescuing, mending, healing, restoring whatever *Gestalten* can be saved.

The moral corruption present in the novel is not always so crass and obvious as in the preceding examples, nor is it always set into distant time and space, but it appears as incipient and pernicious even among some persons tangentially connected with the *Rosenhaus*. Some of Risach's acquaintances, who are not malevolent, nevertheless fall into sins such as complacency, negligence, or passion, which cause the deterioration of things within their keeping and bring about an imbalance or shriveling of their souls. Complacency or negligence, described by Risach as "die *Sünde* der Erfolggenügsamkeit oder der Fahrlässigkeit", is taken very seriously by him as the cause of greatest evil: "Ich glaube, daß sie die größten Uebel gestiftet hat" (VI, 103); and passions, too, are ignoble because any excessive desires hinder our appreciation of the world outside ourselves. "Aber wenn ein Uebermaß von Wünschen und Begehrungen in uns ist, so hören wir nur diese immer an und vermögen nicht die Unschuld der Dinge außer uns zu fassen" (VI, 235).

While Risach's close friends are full-dimensional and deeply felt characters, the more questionable acquaintances are flat and roughly sketched, like caricatures. The author does not treat them with the respect which, according to the ethics of the novel itself, is due every thing and every person. His disparaging attitude conveys the intention to slight these characters and to discourage us from regarding them as noteworthy. As Marianne Thalmann pointed out, Stifter excludes the pathological from the realm of pure being: "Das Pathologische an sich, das wir uns groß oder doch wenigstens interessant zu nennen gewöhnt haben, ist für ihn keine Seinssphäre."[18] Certainly, deficient or warped characters do not truly belong to the *Nachsommer*-realm, for they show man in distortion.

In evaluating the minor characters we must pay close attention to the objects around them, for as Karlheinz Rossbacher has pointed out, each person in *Der Nachsommer* has a "Dingsphäre" which characterizes him.[19] We must also tune our ear to the syntax and sound of the author's description, for Stifter's nuances are revealing. Finally we must hold the characters up against the ideal characters for comparison. Although superficially the non-*Gestalten* have certain traits in common with the main characters, essentially the two types are worlds apart. The discussion will show that the former are not what they seem at first to be, but in the climate of *Der Nachsommer*, which is both serene and rigorous, they are exposed as fools.

A distant cousin of Mathilde is, like Risach, a collector: "Er hatte Münzen, er hatte Siegel, er hatte keltische und römische Alterthümer, Musikgeräthe, Tulpen und Georginen, Bücher, Gemälde und Bildsäulen" (VII, 247 f.). The itemization, however, is so haphazard that we sense there is no order and organization in the collection; that it is, in fact, no collection at all, but a random conglomeration of unrelated items. In the novel, where persons and objects are essentially interrelated, the lack of orderliness here implies a certain chaos, or at least disorderliness, in the character of the collector.

Next to his house he has had a huge concrete plaza with stone steps constructed ("eine große Fläche, die er mit Steinen pflasterte und von welcher künstliche steinerne Stufen in mehreren Richtungen nach dem Garten hinab gingen," VII, 248), where he has placed marble statues for display. His greatest pleasure is to walk back and forth on the pavement to look at the statues, even when it is so hot that the soles of his feet burn: "Das that er auch oft, wenn die heißeste Sonne am Himmel stand und das Pflaster in die Sohlen brannte" (VII, 248). His promenades on the burning concrete show a disregard for his own well-being, similar to the disregard he shows for the organizational needs of his collected objects. The author, who on another occasion speaks out strongly against self-infliction of pain or bodily abuse for the sake of an art object,[20] implies here that the collector's art-appreciation is out of bounds. We might even infer that a cult of art, such as carried on by the collector, has a streak of masochism.

We learn little about this cousin except that he has no children, no close relatives, and no friends to whom he might bequeath his possessions. The sterility of his emotional life indicated by his lack of human contacts is reflected in the unnatural concrete structure with its stone steps in the garden, as his confused inner state is reflected in his disorganized collection.

An old widow who lives with her daughter in an apartment at court seems at first glance to have achieved an admirable peace of mind. She has detached herself from the disturbing events of the day and has disengaged herself from the glittering activities at court: "Es geht Vieles auf dem großen Hofe vor, ich achte nicht darauf" (VI, 219). Life to her is a continual repetition of the same occurrences passing by in eternal flux: "wie bedeutende Dinge da auch vorgehen, so wiederholen sich doch immer die nämlichen, wenn man viele Jahre zuschaut; und endlich schaut man gar nicht mehr zu und hat herinnen ein Buch oder sein Strickzeug, wenn draußen in das Gewehr gerufen wird oder Reiter zu hören sind oder Wagen rollen" (VI, 219 f.). One might suppose, at first, that this widow has reached that ideal contemplative state, that "Einerlei" which in another context, is said to encompass the all;[21] yet by comparing her with another widow, a *Fürstin* whom Heinrich much admires, it becomes clear that the monotonous existence of the old widow is devoid of both contemplation and content, encompassing nothing but the void.

While the retired widow lives in seclusion, the elderly *Fürstin* in the city still receives many visits of "blühende Söhne, schöne Enkel und Enkelinnen," and she enjoys the companionship of a young woman "von außerordentlicher Begabung." Her soirées, where she takes an active part in discussions on world events, politics, literature, and art, attract the most illustrious personages (VII, 53—57). The old widow, by contrast, looks upon court life as a meaningless, transitory illusion, but has found nothing better to take its place. Closed in upon herself, she passes the time with her knitting, or a card game, or with a book — no title is given, so we assume that any book will do. She remembers that Risach was important to her in her youth, but now she has lost all connection with him, as she has lost connection with life itself. Shutting out the world, she has acquired no higher wisdom; with so little interest in anything, she seems spiritually more dead than alive.

The Priest of Rohrberg is introduced by Risach most respectfully as "der hochwürdige Pfarrer von Rohrberg" (VI, 80). Since he is a representative of the church, one might expect that he would be an exemplary character, yet such is not the case. He seeks shelter at the *Rosenhaus* for the same reason as Heinrich: both men fear the outbreak of a severe storm. The forecast is wrong because it fails to take into account certain minute signals of nature which are unmistakable to one who understands nature intimately. Only Risach lives in such close rapport with nature that he can interpret correctly all the atmospheric and biological signs indicating weather changes. While Heinrich is still young enough to slough off bookishness and artificiality that obstruct direct access to nature, the Priest of Rohrberg is no longer likely to reach a healthy accord with the natural scheme of things. The degenerative disease gout, to which he has succumbed, is symptomatic of his general decadence.

Among the secondary characters introduced in the chapter "Das Fest," young Tillburg, "der schlanke Mann mit den lebhaften dunkeln Augen" (VII, 230), appears to be a suitor of Natalie. We learn almost nothing about him directly, but must evaluate him on the basis of information given about his parents. His mother, Lady Tillburg, is a society matron who loves traveling, entertaining, and acquiring whatever is fashionable, luxurious, and beautiful ("Sie hatte sich mit allen Annehmlichkeiten und mit Allem, was prächtig war, umringt" VII, 229). Lord Tillburg does not share her interests, but allows his wife to indulge her fancy in collecting items, which she then scatters about ("zerstreut") in her home. Lord Tillburg, described favorably as "ein schöner alter Herr" (VII, 228) and "der Mann mit dem freundlichen Angesichte" (VII, 230), is of a gentle nature and free from passions. He is permitted the privilege of escorting Mathilde out into the garden, a distinction which undeniably gives him a certain high status.

One circumstance, however, indicates a serious flaw in Tillburg. Although he manages his estate well, he has in recent times had his castle whitewashed. The whitewashing was an aesthetic blunder that illustrates the Tillburgs' lack of taste. Heinrich recoils from the memory of the stark white castle standing against the green background of trees. The castle contrasts so harshly against the blue of the distant mountains and the sky that these look "beinahe finster" (VII, 231). The aesthetic deficiency of this family is matched by a biological deficiency. Lady Tillburg is an only daughter — her brother died very young "in der zartesten Jugend" (VII, 230); Lord Tillburg was the only child of wealthy parents; the marriage between the two produced only one offspring. Since the author stresses the lack of fecundity, as well as the affluence of this family, we may infer that over the generations, luxury and wealth have debilitated the members of this family both physically and spiritually. Young Tillburg does not seem a suitable husband for Natalie, whose nature is unspoiled and vital.

The owner of Haßberg, on the contrary, is extremely energetic. He carries on many of the same practical pursuits as Risach and engages in them with a passion. The syntax describing his activities reveals what is significant about him and conveys the author's opinion of him. A factual and neutral beginning — "In Weißbach hat er schon mehrere Bauten aufgeführt" — leads into a very full sentence which enumerates beneficial projects but produces a stuffed sentence whose overload is the syntactical sign of Haßberg's excessive activity: "In Haßberg richtete er eine Musterwirthschaft ein, er verbesserte die Felder und Wiesen und friedigte sie mit schönen Hecken ein, er errichtete einen auserlesenen Viehstand und führt in geschützten Lagen den Hopfenbau ein, der sich unter seine Nachbarn verbreitete und eine Quelle des Wohlstandes eröffnete" (VII, 231).

The list of activities continues in increasingly breathless haste and culminates in an element that does not bring a stop but suggests endlessness, opening out to an infinity of further remodeling: "Er dämmte dem Ritflusse Wiesen ab, er mauerte die Ufer des Mühlbaches heraus, er baute eine Flachsröstanstalt, baute neue Ställe, Scheuern, Trockenhäuser, Brücken, Stege, Gartenhäuser und ändert im Innern des Schlosses beständig um" (VII, 231). As we see here, the hyperactive Haßberg is not a free man, but one possessed. He is "einer jener Männer, die immer erfinden und bauen *müssen*" (VII, 231). While Risach respects his enterprise and determination ("Unser Freund hält in diesen Dingen große Stücke auf ihn" VII,

232), it is not likely that Risach altogether admires this fanatic, whose life has become quite unbalanced because he carries one inclination to an extreme.

Though the projects individually may be worthwhile, and the urge to build is considered in *Der Nachsommer* to be one of the noblest of human urges, nevertheless even this activity must be kept in proper bounds or it too can produce a disproportionate effect upon man's *Gestalt*. Haßberg's maniacal urge, not only to build, but to change and remodel and reconstruct, may indeed have its roots in a neurosis suggested by his name. His name indicates a basic hostility to nature, which he is ever trying to change, remodel, and in a sense, destroy. The futility of his attempt to assert himself lord over nature is indicated in the image of Haßberg on his deathbed, still planning his next project, but dying nevertheless.

Freiherr von Wachten, however, has no special passions, but husbands his estate efficiently and thereby increases his wealth constantly. His son, another suitor of Natalie, is again an only child. Though no fault in Wachten is mentioned, we learn that on his estate an old castle is crumbling into the dust. Within it are some beautiful sixteenth-century doors which could be renovated and restored to useful purpose, as doors or table tops. Wachten, however, neither reclaims these objects, nor does he sell them to someone who could make use of them, but he allows them to deteriorate, as an old chapel on his estate has already deteriorated.

Of all the guests at the *Sternenhof*, the Ingheim family enjoy the greatest intimacy with Mathilde and Risach. Visits between these two family groups take place several times in the course of the novel's action, and the relationship among them is cordial. The Ingheims appear to be attractive, charming, and successful people, yet already during Heinrich's first meeting with them, he senses that the Ingheim family and the circle around Risach constitute two entirely different categories of human beings. The differences are so pronounced that Heinrich repeats his observation, as if in amazement, "So saßen diese zwei Abtheilungen von Menschen an demselben Tische und bewegten sich in demselben Zimmer, wirklich, zwei Abtheilungen von Menschen" (VI, 286). Later, when he compares the pretty and gracious Ingheim girls with Natalie, he formulates the difference more succinctly: "sie [Natalie] war neben diesen zwei Mädchen *weit höher, wahr, klar* und *schön*, daß jeder Vergleich aufhörte" (VI, 285). The difference between the Ingheims and the élite of the *Rosenhaus* is one of essence. While the Ingheims and other guests live on a plane of high worldly status, the true élite live on the plane of human perfection.

With the Ingheims, there are several small marks of imperfection. As for personal appearance, Heinrich notes that Mrs. Ingheim is somewhat too plump to serve as a model for a work of art; the daughters, though fashionably dressed, do put on too much jewelry (VII, 236). In general, Heinrich finds that the fancy dress of the Ingheims is of lesser quality than that of his friends: "Der geputzte Anzug erschien mir auffallend und unnatürlich, während der andere einfach und zweckmäßig war. Es gewann den Anschein, als ob Mathilde, Natalie, mein alter Gastfreund und selbst Gustav bedeutende Menschen wären, indeß *Jene Einige aus der großen Menge darstellten*, wie sie sich überall befinden" (VI, 284). The characterization of persons by their dress is a frequent occurrence in Stifter's works, as Marianne Ludwig has observed: "Im allgemeinen pflegt Stifter den Menschen durch das Leblose zu charakterisieren, das er an sich hat: die Kleider."[22]

As for the Ingheims' morality, most appalling is their abandonment of an old castle on their estate, and their neglect of a potentially wonderful cactus plant.[23]

In summing up the guests who briefly enter the scene and then disappear from the novel without leaving a trace, it can be said that they have some qualities in common. Fashionable people of the aristocracy or the upper middle class, they have achieved wordly success through efficient management of their properties and by their attainment of certain cultural refinements. Their attitude toward objects of art and beauty is acquisitive rather than formative, however; they collect things for fun, as "Liebhabereien," not out of devotion. They are not inspired to raise beautiful objects to the highest potential of their inherent splendor, nor are they challenged by the objects to improve themselves. Their estates and the furnishings and entertainment in their homes keep them too busy to develop their own beings. Compared to Risach, the men from outside lack abundance of wisdom and vitality; compared to Natalie and Mathilde the other women lack the vigorous radiance of classical beauty. Stifter uses the factor of their low biological fertility to reflect their spiritual effeteness, and his mode of presenting them, deliberately mirrors, in its superficiality, the shallowness of their lives.

It is finally one particular object, one particular *Gestalt*, which pronounces judgment upon the people, while *they* appear to be adjudging *it*. The occasion for the *Fest* at the *Sternenhof* is the partial removal of whitewash from the exterior walls of the castle, a project so important that even its partial completion calls for a celebration. Both Mathilde and Risach find that the whitewash which was applied to the castle by previous owners is irritating and repulsive because, according to Risach, a venerable old castle covered with white is as incongruous as an old woman dressed in white. Accordingly, the time-consuming and costly project of scraping off the lime is undertaken by Risach and his men, while Mathilde watches the emerging of the finer condition with joy. Heinrich recognizes immediately from the distance that the section of newly bared wall is a remarkable improvement ("um Außerordentliches besser," VII, 226). It seems to him "das Natürlichste" (VII, 239). Later he gives a reason for his judgment, which first was intuitive; the castle is a monument ("Denkmal"), and because the material of any monument expresses its character, it should not be overlaid with something foreign. He states his conviction in absolute terms; relative concepts, such as taste, personal preference, or changing fashions do not enter his consideration at all. Subjective judgments and relative truth and pragmatic philosophy have no place in this very objective, uncompromising work. The philosophy underlying it is one that claims absolute validity, as Eric Blackall has noted: "There is only one outlook on life in this book — that which Stifter conceived to be the ideal outlook."[24]

The guests, however, are more uncertain and hesitant in their opinions. Some say that it is a matter of personal taste; some say that fashions change and at times it is better to have a painted castle and at other times it is better to expose the bare rocks; some prefer the naked rock because it looks very special and unique ("etwas Besonderes, etwas sehr Eigenes" VII, 238), some prefer the whitened walls because they look so cheerful ("sehr freundlich" VII, 238). Their opinions either clash with those of the owners, or, where they coincide, the reasons given by the guests are not good reasons.

At Heinrich's marriage the restoration of the original state of the castle is complete ("[Der Sternenhof] stand in seiner reinen ursprünglichen Gestalt da," VIII, 232), as perfect in its way as the marble statue liberated from its disfiguring encasement. Heinrich's judgment was correct because his aesthetic sense is reliable; the opinions of the guests were faulty because they have no sure criterion, no philosophy upon which to base their judgment. They do not grasp a fundamental aesthetic principle, namely that the appearance of an object should express its inherent character. Whatever intuitive aesthetic sense they may once have possessed has been erased by the corrosive effect of their worldliness. Devoid of a definite pure *Gestalt* themselves, they fail to sense the quality of the *Gestalten* around them.

The general insufficiency of the guests is most strikingly illustrated in the garden scene in the presence of the marble grotto nymph. They talk about the art work but have nothing significant to say ("nur allgemeine Dinge" VII, 234). While inconsequential remarks are being exchanged, the sculptured nymph, serene and self-contained, rests in a quiet eternal realm of everflowing water: "Diese ruhte indessen in ihrer Lage, und die Quelle rann sanft und stetig fort" (VII, 234). The white purity of the nymph puts the gaudily clad people to shame. To Heinrich the sight of the socialites chattering irreverently in the presence of a beautiful *Gestalt* is offensive, and he withdraws into silence: "Mir kam es fremd vor, die geputzten Menschen in den verschiedenfarbigen Kleidern vor dem reinen, weißen, weichen Marmor stehen zu sehen. Roland und ich sprachen nichts" (VII, 234).

The decadence of the affluent guests before the garden nymph is sharply apparent when we consider, by comparison, a certain encounter of simple peasants with a work of art, as Risach relates the incident: In the presence of a marble statue of a sleeping youth, the country folk respond instinctively to the beauty of the work by walking on tiptoe, an expression of reverence which impresses Risach: "Eine so unmittelbare und tiefe Anerkennung ist wohl selten einem Meister zu theil geworden" (VII, 89). According to Risach, any sound human being, whether he is sophisticated or ingenuous, must recognize beauty and react to it, if his mind is well-balanced and his emotions receptive, because beauty is a tremendous force: "die große Gewalt, die solche Kunstwerke auf den ebenmäßig gebildeten Geist ausüben, eine Gewalt, die in ihrer Wirkung bei einem Menschen, wenn er altert, nicht abnimmt, sondern wächst, und darum ist es für den in der Kunst Gebildeten, so wie für den völlig Unbefangenen, wenn sein Gemüth nur überhaupt dem Reize zugänglich ist, so leicht, solche Kunstwerke zu erkennen" (VII, 88 f.). The guests at the *Sternenhof* take notice of the magnificent marble nymph, but they are not moved. Their imperviousness to the power of beauty indicates, according to Risach's theory, an unbalanced mind or an unfeeling heart, or at any rate the impairment of aesthetic reflexes, which function naturally in every uncorrupted person.

By showing that these members of the aristocracy and wealthy middle class lack what is basic to a true human being, namely responsiveness to beauty, the author indicts them individually and as a class. While we might be tempted to overlook their individual flaws and failings as inconsequential, because the cliché "nobody is perfect" is comforting to ourselves as well as seemingly charitable to others, Stifter is less tolerant and compromising with his characters in *Der Nachsommer*. Where he registers a fault, it is to be regarded as a sign of basic inadequacy, of failure to live according to the ideal of *Humanität*.

The fault that is present in all the fools in the novel is indifference to the *Gestalt*-principle, which demands ethical and aesthetic flawlessness of everything and of everyone. Technically, the fools in the novel function as warnings against negligence, indifference, and extremes, for the author metes out to them an adverse fate brought on inevitably by their particular sins. Dismaying as these eccentric, shallow, or mediocre characters are, their presence directs us to seek satisfaction in the contemplation of the superior figures.

Oddly enough, the flawlessness of Stifter's ideal human *Gestalten* does not seem affected, unnatural, or forced, but easy, graceful, and natural, although we might not go so far as Otto Stoessl in declaring them absolutely venerable and credible.[25] Joseph Michels describes them more acceptably as myths: as "pure beings" dwelling in the land of the soul, "die reinen Gestalten, ... die nur dem unwirklich sind, der nicht das Wunder des Ewigen ahnend begreift."[26]

The *Gestalt*-principle is the basic measure of man in *Der Nachsommer*, and the test of his *Humanität*. In the light of this principle the salubrity of the ideal beings and the frailties of the fools are revealed. A person rises to transcendence or falls into decadence according to the degree of his effort and success in attaining perfect ethical and aesthetic form.[27]

IX

CONCLUSION

HEINRICH'S PROGRESS TOWARD THE *MARMORGESTALT*

The *Marmorgestalt* as the symbol of eternal verities stands motionless and changeless in the center of the novel. Balancing the staticity of this primary image, Heinrich Drendorf, the questing protagonist, undergoes a process of change and growth. He is not so much a *Gestalt*, as a *Gestaltung*. The other people of the inner circle "stellen alle ein Grund- und Wesensbild des Menschlichen...dar" while Heinrich himself is shown in a process, "wie er leise und organisch immer tiefer in die Idee hineinwächst."[1]

His image never becomes as distinct as that of the other persons or things because of the *Ich*-form of the narrative, which draws the reader into Heinrich's subjectivity and precludes his being viewed from the outside as an object. Still, the narrative point of view, while technically subjective, gives little direct access to Heinrich's stream of consciousness. Heinrich exercises restraint in exposing his inner life just as he ever refrains from tactlessly invading the privacy of other persons. Insights into his emotional states are given rarely and only indirectly, through nature descriptions or silence or gestures. Heinrich does not probe or pry into his inner life but records only such events, thoughts, and feelings as would be standard and acceptable for any proper young man.

The presentation of Heinrich, narrator-protagonist, is then neither objectively nor subjectively revealing. His figure lacks distinctive contours as well as psychological complexity. Although the novel purports to be the record of Heinrich's experiences, it is not the presentation of Heinrich's individuality nor its encounter with external events that sustains the reader's interest. Heinrich is too rational and his *Bildungsweg* is too programmatic for such involvement on the part of the reader. Essentially unproblematical, Heinrich and his *Bildungsweg* are not "interesting," in the usual sense of the word. Nevertheless, the process of gradual unfoldment, development, toward pure being holds its own fascination. Heinrich's *Bildungsweg* is remarkable as an ideal *Gestaltung*.

Like his predecessor, Wilhelm Meister, he is a wanderer, but unlike the former, Heinrich Drendorf never really loses his footing. He proceeds with caution and foresight, never straying from the main course, although he follows some bypaths. His mode of progress is symbolically described in the early pages of the novel:

> Ich ging den Thälern entlang, selbst wenn sie von meiner Richtung abwichen und allerlei Windungen verfolgten. Ich suchte nach solchen Abschweifungen immer meinen Hauptweg wieder zu gewinnen. Ich stieg auch auf Bergjoche und ging auf der entgegengesetzten Seite wieder in das Thal hinab. Ich erklomm manchen Gipfel und suchte, von ihm die Gegend zu sehen und auch schon die Richtung zu erspähen, in welcher ich in nächster Zeit vordringen würde. Im Ganzen hielt ich mich stets, soweit es anging, nach dem Hauptzuge des Gebirges und wich von der Wasserscheide so wenig, als möglich, ab. (VI, 32)[2]

He ascends the highest mountains and penetrates the fields of science, philosophy, sociology, and art. He probes the nature of existence to the very frontier of death and meaninglessness. Though terrified in the face of the void, he resists the seduction of despair by summoning up the forms he has come to love. He becomes visibly more knowledgeable, wiser, more loving, and more aware, as he reaches out into ever more distant regions and returns to his home enriched. Gradually the central point from which he starts on his expeditions shifts from his home to the *Rosenhaus*, which becomes "Mitte des gesamten in diesem Roman gestalteten Bildungsvorgangs."[3]

Despite Heinrich's sensible approach to life, there is an element of the irrational in his *Bildungsweg*. An inner urge ("ein gewisser

Drang meines Herzens" VI, 11) starts him off on a career in general science ("zu einem Wissenschafter [sic] im Allgemeinen"). This ambition to acquire full knowledge about the earth through scientific investigation indicates a presumptuousness ("Ungeheuerlichkeit" VI, 11) not without a Faustian hubris.

His early progress comes about through his own efforts, with guidance from his father and instruction from his tutors. While learning from books and observation, he shows from the start a predilection for shapes and configurations in mathematics, mineralogy, botany, and biology. Fascinated by lines and structures, he becomes convinced that form is the essential differentiating characteristic of all phenomena. Thereupon he sets up his own cataloging system, whereby he groups objects according to their total *Gestalt* rather than according to any special characteristics, as was customary.

The objects of his studies, the things themselves, seem to lead him on to further investigations.[4] After he has learned a great deal about the formations and the geological conditions of the mountains, he feels a sense of accomplishment. His self-satisfaction is apparent in his first meeting with Risach, master of the *Rosenhaus*, when he introduces himself as "beinahe eine Art Naturforscher" (VI, 49), a prideful statement which he later has cause to regret.

From the moment of Heinrich's entry into the *Rosenhaus*, his being is challenged by the stimulating atmosphere there and by the personality of Risach, who has established such a rich and austere order. Risach is the most interesting character within the novel, because with him *Gestalt* has turned into deed, and the magnitude of his perfection has assumed form in magnitude of vital activity.

Early in childhood Risach shows a strong liking for concrete forms. He looks at cakes of ice floating in the river, he watches trees being felled, huts being built, boards being nailed together (VIII, 81). As a little boy he puts all kinds of things together, fashioning here a city, there a person, and there an object to represent an abstract concept (VIII, 82). Later his *Gestalt* inclination is an obstacle to his success in the diplomatic field. Because he regards each state as a *Gestalt* with its own intrinsic value and need, he seeks no advantages for his own state, but aims at benefits for each separate state. His career is rich in honor, but it does not satisfy him because he cannot see the results of his work in tangible form. After his retirement he finds contentment at the *Rosenhaus* where his formative talent expresses itself in the restoration of art objects and the management of his estate. In art as well as life he can now demand not merely forms, but forms of beauty.

In a serious vein he describes his activities as follows: "durch Anschauung hoher Gestalten der Kunst und der Schöpfung... Freude in mein Herz zu sammeln und Freude, Erkenntniß und Verehrung der Gestalten auf meine Mitmenschen zu übertragen" (VIII, 85 f.). More whimsically he characterizes his work as "Blumen zurecht legen" (VIII, 93), an unpretentious image which recalls the arrangement Natalie once makes of a bouquet of field flowers. She does not discard a single flower nor even a blade of grass, but gives to each a meaningful place in the whole and thereby produces a pleasing total effect: "es erschien also, daß sie weniger eine Auslese der Blumen machen, als dem alten Strauße eine neue schönere Gestalt geben wollte" (VII, 213). Risach's endeavor to give to everything and everyone a purposeful place in its environment has produced a community of singular excellence, which, like Natalie's bouquet, is a *Gestalt* of beauty.

Nameless through most of the book because one name cannot encompass his universality, Risach is protector, gardener, farmer, artist, teacher, friend, priest. He has overcome passion and personal identity, which lie in the past and are revealed only when the past is unfurled. His life is totally absorbed by service: "im Dienen an dem, was des Bleibens wert ist, wie immer es auch sich darbieten möge, ob Tier und Pflanze, Stein, Buch, Geräth und Kunstwerk."[5] The *Rosenhaus* is a manifestation of Risach's spirit.

The *Rosenhaus* does not offer Heinrich anything really new, for already in his childhood home there are fine paintings, beautiful furnishings, good books, excellent specimens of Greek art, a wise elderly man, a kindly gracious lady, a lovely young girl. Still, it is at the *Rosenhaus*, stimulated by Risach's example and guided by his counsel, that Heinrich acquires insight into the value of the things that have always been around him. One of his basic experiences is the sudden realization that something which he has heretofore not heeded is actually of great significance, like the mountain range, which in his childhood seems of little import ("dieses kleine blaue Fleckchen" VI, 29) but later becomes crucial to his development. When shown Risach's furniture, he remembers the furniture in his own home and regrets that he never learned to appreciate it; upon seeing Risach's paintings he becomes aware that his father also has a superb collection; only after the *Marmorgestalt* revelation does he appreciate his father's cameos.

Certain objects in the landscape, previously seen but unnoticed, such as the *Rosenhaus* and the *Sternenhof* with its maple trees, now emerge as important (VI, 316). Faces too become objects of interest to him. He begins to notice the faces of older people after he has met Risach and has attended a performance of *King Lear*. Beautiful young faces begin to engage his attention after he sees Natalie at the theater. Formerly unobservant of girls' faces, Heinrich has difficulty recalling Natalie's features, but remembers her only as "ein unbestimmtes, dunkles Bild von Schönheit" (VI, 217), and it takes several encounters before he recognizes her again. The *Marmorgestalt* is present and visible to Heinrich for years before he becomes receptive to it. The recurring motif of growth in awareness indicates one of the basic ideas of the novel, namely that all of life's riches are available at all times, but one must develop spiritual receptivity to come into their possession. In acquiring perceptivity and sensitivity to what is around him, Heinrich gains in maturity. The individual and the world are seen here to be engaged in a dynamic process of mutual interaction, as Dehn suggests: "Das Vermögen, in diese Welt begreifend immer tiefer einzudringen, bestimmt den Prozeß menschlicher Entfaltung."[6]

Further stimulation is provided for Heinrich by the series of shocks which climax in the *Marmorgestalt*-revelation. As Gerald Gillespie says: "Stifter's purpose is to conduct us toward the higher experience of Platonic astonishment, when everything is transfigured in the shock of recognition."[7] Soon after Heinrich enters the

Rosenhaus he is shocked at his error in mistaking Risach for the gardener instead of recognizing him as the master of the *Asperhof*. His self-assurance receives another jolt when his prediction of a thunderstorm fails to materialize during the night. As the young "scientist" stands corrected by the older man who made no claim to being a scientist, Heinrich humbly admits to being "doch im Grunde nur ein gewöhnlicher Fußreisender" (VI, 132). The disturbing realization that there may be many things yet in heaven and on earth about which he is ignorant quickens his activities, and that summer he begins projects not previously planned (VI, 193).

In attending the performance of *King Lear* Heinrich expects to see "eine erlogene Geschichte" (VI, 208), and instead he is shocked and amazed to experience "die wirklichste Wirklichkeit" (VI, 212). The striking image of destruction given by the horses and the wagon wheels outside the theater ("die Pferde zerstampften und die Räder zerschnitten die sich bildende Eisdecke" VI, 208), applies not only to the fate of Lear and his pride, but also symbolizes the shattering of Heinrich's encrusted complacency. Heinrich, who had approached the theater with the prejudices of a scientist superior to the realm of the imagination now feels himself "zermalmt." Beside himself with pain at the tragedy of the old king, he cannot eat or sleep all night. The shock of realizing his ignorance and misapprehension about the theater and its impact upon the beholder leads him to a serious study of Shakespeare.

One summer, while engaged in geological research, Heinrich becomes beset by questions about the origin and the goal and purpose of life, questions which the scientist cannot answer. Heinrich's inability to cope with the immense mystery of the earth shocks him into awareness of the inadequacy of science in the face of existential problems. Defeated in his attempt to arrive at fundamental truths through scientific data, he turns to the area of art for answers. He makes an attempt to grasp the mountains as a whole *Gestalt* in a landscape painting, but is again defeated. Even his literary efforts fail to capture the essence of the mountains through descriptions of their forms, colors, lights, and shadows (VIII, 28). The nature of existence continues to elude him, even in his aesthetic endeavors.

The thunderstorm does not occur on Heinrich's first visit to the *Rosenhaus*, but instead, during that night a wind rushes through the trees. The whole experience of the *Asperhof* is like a harsh wind challenging Heinrich's being and preparing him for the breakthrough of the real thunderstorm that occurs much later with the *Marmorgestalt*-revelation.

The first time Heinrich sees the *Marmorgestalt* he is impressed only by the unusual glass roof and the play of light on the figure. Somewhat later he notices the fine quality of the marble. A year later he mentions the statue casually in passing by. Again a year later his eyes are suddenly opened and he asks Risach in shocked bewilderment: "Warum habt Ihr mir denn nicht gesagt, ... daß die Bildsäule, welche auf Eurer Marmortreppe steht, so schön ist?" (VII, 75).

While Heinrich moves from the shock of one defeat to the next, he constantly gains deeper insight and stronger motivation. Though Heinrich's presumptuous goal to learn all about the earth proves to be abortive, still it enables him to acquire a great deal of factual information, which opens many doors to him and arouses Natalie's admiration. His geological studies do not specifically solve the problems of existence but do indirectly lead him to the *Rosenhaus*. His opinion, maintained so tenaciously in the argument about the weather, turns out to be embarrassingly erroneous, but meanwhile he has impressed Risach with his conviction and enthusiasm. His defeat in science leads him to art; his unsuccessful landscape painting hastens the *Marmorgestalt*-revelation. The shock treatment he undergoes stimulates him to seek new directions and to exert himself. The desired illumination comes to him finally through the *Marmorgestalt*, which offers the aesthetic vision of a fundamental reality.

Though comforted and gratified by this image of perfect beauty, Heinrich still longs for something unknown which must exist and give meaning to his life (VII, 221). As Faust finds salvation because of his eternal striving and through the grace of God in Gretchen's love, so Heinrich finds his life's fulfillment partly because of his own efforts and through divine grace, here termed "Glück," which Natalie bestows upon him. As alter-image of the *Marmor-*

gestalt, she possesses all the "Herrlichkeit" and "Pracht" of the divine form, and about her there is a special radiance: "ein tiefes Glück" (VI, 285).

Satisfied in his vision and in his "Glück," Heinrich founds a family and enters actively into society, having reached "jene Weltoffenheit, ...die die Vorbedingung ist für jede schöpferische Tätigkeit."[8] Love has brought him to the threshhold of a life of simplicity and stability, to be carried on in the service of mankind.

The *Marmorgestalt* is like a nucleus that holds all the elements of the novel together in its gravitational field. It stands in the middle chapter like a bright and shining central point from which the *Gestalten* of the novel radiate and the whole design of the novel spreads out.

Like the *Marmorgestalt*, there are other points of mysterious significance appearing on the *Bildungsweg* of Heinrich as dots or "white dots," which function both as centers of energy and as vista points. The *Rosenhaus*, perceived first as a "weiße[r] Punkt," is, despite its negligible size ("Wie war nun der Punkt so klein in der großen Welt" VI, 192), a powerful center of force and vision. Here the spark of Risach's genius is transmitted, and from here Heinrich can survey all the *Gestalten* of nature, art, and man in the world.

The cherry tree situated at the highest point of Risach's estate is another such point: "ein dunkler, ausgezeichneter Punkt" (IV, 63), which provides a view of all the land-formations below and offers a retreat for revitalization.

The archetypal white dot in *Der Nachsommer* is the mountain, which Heinrich experiences early in life as a radiant nucleus. The mountain upon which he once stands is like the luminous center in a design on frozen window-panes. Looking down upon manifold configurations, he senses the point on which he stands as a creative and illuminative spark. This point of energy brings forth the configurations of the surrounding landscape and provides the vista point for their contemplation:

> Es kam ein altes Bild, das ich einmal in einem Buche gelesen und wieder vergessen hatte, in meine Erinnerung. Wenn das

> Wasser in unendlich kleinen Tröpfchen, die kaum durch ein Vergrößerungsglas ersichtlich sind, aus dem Dunste der Luft sich auf die Tafeln unserer Fenster absetzt und die Kälte dazu kömmt, die nöthig ist, so entsteht die Decke von Fäden, Sternen, Wedeln, Palmen und Blumen, die wir gefrorene Fenster heißen. Alle diese Dinge stellen sich zu einem Ganzen zusammen, und die Strahlen, die Thäler, die Rücken, die Knoten des Eises sind, durch ein Vergrößerungsglas angesehen, bewunderungswürdig. Eben so stellt sich, von sehr hohen Bergen aus gesehen, die niedriger liegende Gestaltung der Erde dar. Sie muß aus einem erstarrenden Stoffe entstanden sein und streckt ihre Fächer und Palmen in großartigem Maßstabe aus. Der Berg selber, auf dem ich stehe, ist *der weiße, helle und sehr glänzende Punkt*, den wir in der Mitte der zarten Gewebe unserer gefrorenen Fenster sehen. (VI, 39 f.)

The bright creative point in the frozen windows and on the mountain peak objectifies the function of the *Marmorgestalt* in the novel. As the central concept in the author's vision, perfect *Gestalt* is the white point, the spark from which all the forms in the constellation of the novel have emanated. From this center of vision, as from the mountain top, all the surrounding material assumes meaning and significance. The *Marmorgestalt* is the basic idea of the novel made manifest.

NOTES

NOTES: I. INTRODUCTION

THE *MARMORGESTALT* AND THE CONCEPT *GESTALT*

1 Adalbert Stifter, *Der Nachsommer*, ed. Franz Hüller and others, in *Sämmtliche Werke*, VI, VII, VIII[1] (Prag und Reichenberg, 1901 ff.). All parenthetical references to volume and page are to this edition. All italics used have been supplied by me.

2 Max Stefl, "Adalbert Stifters Gestalten," in *Homo homini homo: Festschrift für Joseph Drexel* (München, 1966), p. 27, "Immer wieder dringt für das Schöne, Edle, für das Vollendete, der Begriff Gestalt durch."

3 Attention has been drawn repeatedly to similarities between Stifter's development ideal and the Leibnizian monads. See, for example, Curt Hohoff, *Adalbert Stifter: Seine dichterischen Mittel und die Prosa des neunzehnten Jahrhunderts* (Düsseldorf, 1949), p. 105, "Die weltanschauliche Grundlage solcher Vorstellungen liegt in dem Gedanken einer verwirklichten oder fortschreitenden vernünftigen Harmonie nach den Kategorien von Schönheit, Zweckmäßigkeit und Vollkommenheit, die zum erstenmal bei Leibniz auftaucht und die ästhetisch-religiöse Weltbetrachtung der Aufklärung und Klassik-Romantik begründete."

4 Walter Muschg, "Das Farbenspiel von Stifters Melancholie," *Studien zur tragischen Literaturgeschichte* (Bern, 1965), p. 199, "*Nachsommer* und *Witiko* sind sakrale ... Lehrgedichte, die eine geistige Ordnung darstellen und sie aus hieratischen Sinnbildern aufbauen."

5 Keith Spalding, "Adalbert Stifter," in *German Men of Letters*, V, ed. Alex Natan (London, 1969), p. 196, "Indeed the novel is an illustrated code of law setting out the guide-lines towards the perfect life."

6 Fritz Martini, *Deutsche Literatur im bürgerlichen Realismus 1848—1898. Geschichtliche Darstellungen* V/2 (Stuttgart, 1962), p. 505.

7 "Stifter: *Der Nachsommer*," in *Der deutsche Roman*, ed. Benno von Wiese (Düsseldorf, 1963), II, p. 37, "Die Spannung zwischen dem Leidenschaftlichen als Unruhe, Unsitte, Unform und Unsinn und dem geduldigen Erfahren und Aufweisen des vernünftig schöpferischen Gesetzes wird von Stifter als das große existentielle Kräftespiel verstanden."

8 For a discussion of the struggle between the forces of order and chaos in another work of Stifter's, see J. P. Stern, "Adalbert Stifters ontolo-

gischer Stil," in *Studien und Interpretationen*, ed. Lothar Stiehm (Heidelberg, 1968), pp. 116—119.
9 "Das Farbenspiel von Stifters Melancholie," p. 201. A more negative judgment of Stifter's endeavor to subdue annihilistic forces by overwhelming them with an abundance of things, is given by Max Rychner, who relates the phenomenon to Stifter's reactionary tendencies. See "Stifters *Nachsommer*," in *Deutsche Romane von Grimmelshausen bis Musil*, quoted from *Interpretationen* III, ed. Jost Schillemeit (Frankfurt, a. M., 1966), p. 193, "Die mit vielen Sachen so eifrig aufgebaute Fülle überzeugt zuweilen kaum noch, daß sie mehr sei als mühsam bezwungene, gelegentlich nurmehr verstellte Leere; sie wirkt wie ein verzweifeltes Festhalten von Dingen, die man entgleiten fühlt und im Innersten bereits entglitten weiß. Es ist ein magisches Beschwören, ein großartig tragischer Wille am Werk."
10 *Die Restauration des Schönen: Stifters "Nachsommer*," Germanistische Abhandlungen, No. 6 (Stuttgart, 1965).
11 Curt Hohoff, *Adalbert Stifter: Seine dichterischen Mittel*, p. 110.
12 Wilhelm Dehn, *Ding und Vernunft: Zur Interpretation von Stifters Dichtung*. Literatur und Wirklichkeit, III (Bonn, 1969), pp. 225 f.

NOTES: II

ISOLATION AND DEATH

1 See, for example, Eric Blackall, *Adalbert Stifter: A Critical Study* (Cambridge, Eng., 1948), pp. 311—330. The following statement by Mr. Blackall epitomizes the acclaim which this aspect of the work has received: "The whole power of the work proceeds from its complete, unshaken serenity, its all-pervading harmony, its distinguished simplicity and its spiritualized conception of order — all these are aspects both of the higher life and of the artistic expression which Stifter gives to it" (p. 312).
2 "Gleichwohl ist das Schwermuts- und Todes-Motiv im Werk selbst nur sehr verborgen zwischen den Zeilen und den Sätzen da." Walther Rehm, *Nachsommer. Zur Deutung von Stifters Dichtung* (Bern, München, 1951), p. 31.
3 Friedrich Seebaß, "Über Stifters Dichtung," *Deutsche Rundschau*, LXXVIII (Oct. 1952), 1079.

4 For all the tranquility which the book as a whole exudes, Roy Pascal exaggerates when he states that in *Der Nachsommer* there is "complete lack of incident and accident, tension, struggle, plot" and a "complete absence of internal stress." *The German Novel* (Manchester, 1956), pp. 56 and 60. The tranquility is achieved not through absence of emotional tension, but by the deliberate, calm flow of the style, by the relegation of the more passionate scenes into the past, by the use of images and landscape to suggest states of mind, and by a constant adherence to the highest standards of taste in expression. Roy Pascal himself contradicts the above-quoted statement later in his sensitive analysis of *Der Nachsommer* by finding numerous examples of tension and internal stress in the novel.

5 Adalbert Stifter, *Der Nachsommer*, ed. Franz Hüller and others, in *Sämmtliche Werke*, VI, VII, VIII[1] (Prag und Reichenberg, 1901 ff.). All italics in passages quoted from *Der Nachsommer* in this and subsequent chapters have been added by me.

6 One might take this symbolism to mean that Stifter regarded the institution of the church as another harbinger of culture.

7 Roy Pascal, *The German Novel*, p. 69, has noted the characteristic subtlety with which the author apprises the reader of the love developing between these two people, unknown to themselves, and therefore unknown to the story-teller Heinrich. "We become aware of it only in the most indirect manner, and, being experienced readers of novels, we even know more about it than the story-teller himself. ... Only after the declaration of their love can we interpret his unease, and her restlessness."

8 Pascal, p. 65, attributes Heinrich's withdrawal here merely to his exaggerated concern for "propriety": "when he twice meets Natalie by chance, he urgently seeks to withdraw in order not to offend her; and we feel the offence is more to propriety than to her or to morality." Instead, Heinrich seeks to withdraw on only *one* occasion and only because he is embarrassed at finding her in a condition obviously not intended for the eyes of others. For a discussion of Heinrich's second accidental meeting with Natalie, see below.

9 "Wir machten uns das Vergnügen, Steine ziemlicher Größe von ihr [der Klippe] hinab zu werfen, um den Steinstaub aufwirbeln zu sehen, wenn der Geworfene auf Klippen stieß, und um sein Gepolter in den Klippen und sein Rasseln in dem am Fuße des Felsens befindlichen Gerölle zu hören" (VIII, 159).

10 "In der Nachsommer-Dichtung ist der Tod ... nicht gegenwärtig." Rehm, *Nachsommer*, p. 99.

11 Adolf von Grolman, *Adalbert Stifters Romane* (Halle, 1926), p. 62, "Doch niemand stirbt, nichts stirbt außer den immer wiederkehrenden Rosen, und selten wird der Tod erwähnt."

12 For an excellent study of the importance of the marble muse, see G. Joyce Hallamore, "The Symbolism of the Marble Muse in Stifter's *Nachsommer*," PMLA, LXXIV (1959), 398—405.

13 It is important to be aware of the fact that Stifter frequently uses landscape descriptions to indicate the emotions of his characters, as Franz Matzke has pointed out in *Die Landschaft in der Dichtung Adalbert Stifters* (Eger, 1932), p. 103: "Denn namentlich im *Nachsommer* tritt die Landschaft nicht nur neben den Menschen, sondern unmittelbar an seine Stelle und verkündet in ihrer Sprache, was der Mensch verschweigt. Der Leser muß dann ... das Innere der Menschen aus einer zart hingehauchten Natursymbolik herausfühlen."

14 Stifter's writings abound in idyllic nature descriptions, but his feeling toward nature is not purely one of loving admiration. This episode is an example of what Pascal describes as "evidence of that distrust of nature, of that gnawing uncertainty, which always lowers on the horizon of this apparently soothing book" (p. 70).

15 Reprinted by permission of the editors from PMLA, LXXX (June, 1965), 254—258.

NOTES: III

MATHILDE AND THE ROSES

1 Friedrich Hebbel, *Sämtliche Werke*, ed. R. M. Werner. 1. Abt., XII (Berlin, 1904), 184 [published first in the *Leipziger Illustrierte Zeitung*, 4 Sept. 1858]: "Anfangs schüchtern und durch die Erinnerung an Lessings Laokoon in der behäbigen Entfaltung seiner aufs Breite und Breiteste angelegten Beschreibungsnatur vielleicht noch ein wenig gestört, machte er bald die Erfahrung, daß dieser einst so gefährliche Laokoon in unseren Tagen Niemand mehr schadet, und faßte Muth. Zuerst begnügte er sich, uns die Familien der Blumen aufzuzählen, die auf seinen Lieblingsplätzen gedeihen; dann wurden uns die Exemplare vorgerechnet, und jetzt erhalten wir das Register der Staubfäden.... Was wird hier nicht alles weitläuftig betrachtet und geschildert; es fehlt nur noch die Betrachtung der Wörter, womit man schildert, und die Schilderung der Hand, womit man diese Betrachtung niederschreibt, so ist der Kreis vollendet. Ein Inventar ist eben so interessant, und wenn die Gerichtsperson, die es abfaßt, ihr

Signalement hinzufügt, so sind auch alle Elemente dieser sogenannten Erzählung beisammen."

2 See Konrad Steffen, *Adalbert Stifter: Deutungen* (Basel, 1955), p. 225, "Der *Nachsommer* ist ein Rosenbuch: Rosen blühen im Garten zu Heinbach, in Risachs Park, an seinem Haus, im Sternenhof, in Drendorfs Garten, sie blühen in den Gesprächen und in den farbigen Abbildungen der Rosenbücher; ja selbst die schmiedeisernen Ornamente an den Fenstern des Asperhofes haben Rosengestalt." Paul Requadt, *Das Sinnbild der Rosen in Stifters Dichtung: Zur Deutung seiner Farbensymbolik*, Akademie der Wissenschaften und der Literatur, Abhandlungen der Klasse der Literatur, no. 2 (Mainz-Wiesbaden, 1952), also regards the roses as one of the few central symbols of Stifter's entire literary work ("Eins der wenigen Kernsymbole seiner Dichtung" p. 18).

3 Adalbert Stifter, *Der Nachsommer*, ed. Franz Hüller and others, in *Sämmtliche Werke*, VI, VII, VIII[1] (Prag und Reichenberg, 1901 ff.).

4 Note the following passages: "Die Rücksicht der Anpflanzung schien nur die zu sein, daß in der Rosenwand *keine Unterbrechung* stattfinden möge" (VI, 45); "daß sich *keine leere Stelle* an der Wand des Hauses zeigte" (VI, 158); "bis sich die Wand allgemach *erfüllte*" (VI, 152).

5 In *Der Nachsommer* such characteristics are best exhibited by the *Marmorgestalt* (see Chapter I, p. 16); it exercises a formative influence upon anyone in its vicinity; as Heinrich says, sensing the beneficent power of the muse: "Was ist der Mensch, und *wie hoch wird er*, wenn er in solcher Umgebung, und zwar in solcher Umgebung von größerer Fülle, weilen darf" (VIII, 63).

6 The preparatory beds for the plants are called "schools"; when the plants become "ill," they are placed back in the garden, "gleichsam in das Rosenhospital"; an injured stem has its "wounds bandaged" (VI, 155). Death comes finally to the roses, says Risach, as it comes to every living being.

7 "Sie hat Schmerzen und Kummer ertragen; aber sie hat *Alles Gott geopfert* und hat gesucht, mit sich in das Gleiche zu kommen, sie ist mit den Menschen gut gewesen, und jetzt ist sie *in tiefem Glücke*" (VII, 176).

8 Cf. Konrad Steffen, p. 237, "[Die Rosen] sind Urbilder, sind Rosen, die — mit Angelus Silesius zu reden — 'von Ewigkeit in Gott also geblüht' haben."

9 VIII, 115. Note also the awkwardness of the clumsy carps, which reflects the ineptitude of Risach's behavior throughout the Mathilde incident. (All future references in the discussion of the flash-back episode of Volume VIII[1] will be given by page number only.)

10 On Risach's estate it is a rule that roses must never be cut or broken off (VI, 292). Heinrich himself never breaks this rule. When his sister Klotilde on one occasion gives him a rose she has broken off, she

receives not thanks but reproof from her brother ("Ich nahm die Rose und sagte, Klotilde würde meinem Gastfreunde einen *schlechten Dienst* tun, wenn sie in seinem Garten eine Rose pflückte" VII, 324). Here, too, the apparently minor infringement of a rule has serious implications. Through the sympathizing concern of Mrs. Drendorf the author points to something unhealthy in Klotilde's strong emotional attachment to her brother ("Klotilde wird die Art ihrer Neigung zu Dir umwandeln müssen, und möge das Alles mit gelindem Kelche vorüber gehen" VII, 324). In the evening before Klotilde is informed of her brother's engagement, the atmosphere is disturbingly foreboding ("Auch hatte man heute in dem lauen Abende mehrere der Glasabtheilungen geöffnet, der Eppich flüsterte in einem gelegentlichen Luftzuge, und die Flamme im Innern der Lampe wankte unerfreulich" VII, 326). After the disclosure, Klotilde rushes into her brother's room, greatly upset. Hurt and jealous, she cries out that her heart, which she had wanted to bring her brother, is broken.

[11] See, e.g., Eric Blackall, *Adalbert Stifter* (Cambridge, Eng., 1948), p. 324, "There is never the slightest shade of violence, extravagance or overstatement. The sentences move with the same measured composure as the characters. It is distinguished, stately, leisurely language which never makes the slightest compromise with slang or jargon, never approaches anywhere near the *cliché* or the colloquial."

[12] Cf. Paul Requadt, *Das Sinnbild der Rosen in Stifters Dichtung*, p. 34, "Diese Szene zeigt charakteristische Züge seines frühen Stils, sie kommt geradezu einem Selbstzitat gleich. Dieser vom Dichter offenbar beabsichtigte 'Stilbruch' trennt die ekstatische und vom Dämonischen berührte Liebesbegegnung von dem übrigen Roman."

[13] Paul Requadt, developing his thesis that in Stifter's works the color red always signifies the presence of a nonrational force which he terms "das Dämonische," finds the "Dämonie des Rot" especially prevalent in the Risach-Mathilde episode, where it may be said to constitute the "Leitfarbe" (pp. 24 f.).

[14] Cf. Joachim Müller, *Adalbert Stifter* (Halle, 1956), p. 22, "In Risachs Jugendgeschichte schafft die Leidenschaft erst *unergründlichste Glückseligkeit*, aber sie überflutet alles Maß und verzehrt die ihr Verfallenen, so daß Leidenschaft selbst den zauberhaften Bund wieder zerstört."

[15] See n. 5 above for characteristics of perfect forms.

[16] Cf. Steffen, p. 221, "Es gehört zum polaren Aufbau des *Nachsommers*, daß sich von der Gestaltenwelt im Rosenhaus, im Sternenhof und im Kaufmannshause die Gestaltlosigkeit jener Scheinwelt abhebt, welche einst die junge Mathilde für sich und ihren Geliebten erträumt hat. ... Hier wird die Welt nicht mit den beobachtenden Augen Heinrichs, des Naturforschers, aufgenommen. Sie 'schwimmt' vielmehr vor dem

Blick der jugendlich Liebenden; die festgegründete Erde gerät ins 'Fließen'."

17 "Es war, als blühten und glühten alle Rosen um das Haus, obwohl nur die grünen Blätter und die Ranken um dasselbe waren" (VIII, 133).

18 Risach's excessive despair, which later culminates in a near-attempt at suicide, can be regarded as a natural consequence of his abdication of self to passion. See Müller, p. 102: "Wie bezeichnend, daß die Lebenssituation, die mit der leidenschaftlichen Aufwallung des Herzens, mit der blinden, unbedingten und ausschließlichen Übermächtigung des Ich begann, in die radikale Verzweiflung mündet, die keinen anderen Ausweg zu finden glaubt als den Selbstmord."

19 Here again passion itself destroys love and happiness. Cf. Müller, p. 104, "Wen das Feuer der Leidenschaft ergriffen hat, dem muß jedes Maß entfallen, und jedes gerechte Abwägen liegt ihm fern. Erschütternd die nur zu grausamer Selbstpeinigung führende Anklage Mathildens, die allein in ihrer Leidenschaftsliebe atmen zu können glaubt; in der schmerzvollen Empörung ob des jäh zerstörten Bundes vermag sie weder den Eltern noch dem Geliebten Gerechtigkeit widerfahren zu lassen." See also Roy Pascal, *The German Novel* (Manchester, 1956), p. 55. "Her error, touching in its natural violence, is deliberately intended to indicate the unreliability of the impulsive heart, which destroys its own happiness."

20 For a sensitive stylistic analysis of this conversation, see Walther Rehm, *Nachsommer* (Bern-München, 1951), p. 64.

21 The thesis that suffering can bring about extraordinary beauty is also illustrated by some crippled alder trees on Risach's estate, which do not achieve normal development because they grow in a swampy meadow. Through their tortuous growth, wood is produced which is beautiful and very valuable for cabinets, because the grain shows "die schönste Gestaltung von Farbe und Zeichnung in Ringen, Flammen und allerlei Schlangenzügen" (VI, 147). This wood is "außerordentlich, so feurig und fast erhaben" (VI, 323).

22 "Eine schöne Rose... von vorzüglich leichter Arbeit und... ihrem Vorbilde treuer, als ich irgendwo in Eisen gesehen hatte" (VII, 126).

23 See Pascal, p. 55, "The theme of [the story of Risach and Mathilde] is, in the main, the transmission of their wisdom to the young pair, Heinrich and Natalie."

24 "Natalie ist... befestigt, veredelt und geglättet worden" (VIII, 173); "Theils durch eine sehr sorgfältige Erziehung ist mehr Ruhe und Stetigkeit in ihr Dasein gekommen" (VIII, 172).

25 Natalie, sharing in the perfection of the *Marmorgestalt*, embodies ideal human qualities so fully that she may be regarded as the archetype of human perfection. See Konrad Steffen, p. 238, "Vollkommener und kraftvoller als alle übrigen Gestalten im *Nachsommer* ist Natalie. Sie ist

'unermeßlich schön', ist ungewordene, urbildliche Schönheit in Menschengestalt, ohne Vergleich in ihrer Zeit."
26 See Walther Rehm, p. 63, "Pflege der Rose ist — *sub rosa* und aus der Tiefe der Zeit — Pflege der Liebe."
27 Reprinted by permission of the editors from PMLA, LXXXI (Oct., 1966), 400—408.

NOTES: IV

THE *CEREUS PERUVIANUS*

1 Adalbert Stifter, *Der Nachsommer*, ed. Franz Hüller and others, in *Sämmtliche Werke*, VI, VII, VIII[1] (Prag und Reichenberg, 1901 ff.).
2 The word *Gestalt* itself is used 310 times in the novel; the derivative *Gestaltung* 67 times. It differs from the synonyms *Ding, Sache, Objekt, Gegenstand* in that it contains the concept of "form," both external (physical) and internal (spiritual) form. The importance of this concept dawns upon the reader, as upon Heinrich, only gradually. Cf. Konrad Steffen, *Adalbert Stifter. Deutungen* (Basel, 1955), p. 223: "Gestalt ist eines der wichtigsten Worte im *Nachsommer*. ... Jung und unerfahren spricht Heinrich noch von 'wunderlichen Gestalten.' Erst viel später lernt er empfinden, wie wunderbar sie sind, wie wunderbar Gestalten überhaupt sein können." See also p. 237: "sein [Stifters] künstlerisches Anliegen ... gilt der Gestalt in ihrer letzten Erlesenheit und Steigerung: dem Urbild."
3 Compare Heinrich's observation of the stimulating and ennobling effect of the statue (VIII, 63).
4 "Was die Gärtnerleute anbelange, so verändern sich diese schon seit mehreren Jahren gar nicht mehr" (VI, 227). Heinrich himself achieves immutability only after his wedding, when Risach marks the completion of his development with the pronouncement, "Ihr werdet Euch nicht ändern" (VIII, 174).
5 Heinrich's sudden discomposure at this announcement ("Ich sah ihn befremdet an" VIII, 225) is a dissonant note, unexplained by the author. Can it be that Heinrich hears Simon's statement as a presumptuously familiar allusion to the bliss that awaits him on this wedding night when the bride will "reward" him for his "goodness"? Such an allusion would,

of course, be out of the question with the gardener, but thoughts of an erotic nature may well be in the mind of Heinrich on this occasion and could be betrayed by just such a slip in rational perception.

6 Heinrich Teutschmann, *Adalbert Stifters gegenwärtiges Wort* (Dornach [Schweiz], 1967), p. 70, refers to Natalie as "Heldin und Heilige" and points out that "mit dem weihnachtlichen Namen... (festum natale)... Natalie — ist das Weihnachtserlebnis der Kinder in 'Bergkristall,' in die Existenz der Erwachsenen erhoben."

7 For an exploration of the symbolic quality of colors in Stifter's works (especially the color red) see Paul Requadt, *Das Sinnbild der Rosen in Stifters Dichtung. Zur Deutung seiner Farbensymbolik*, Akademie der Wissenschaften und der Literatur, Abhandlungen der Klasse der Literatur, no. 2 (Mainz-Wiesbaden, 1952).

8 Eric Blackall, *Adalbert Stifter* (Cambridge, Eng., 1948), p. 100. See also p. 17.

9 Reprinted by permission of the editors from *The German Quarterly*, XL (November, 1967), 664—672. Previously an abstract of the chapter was read at the Pacific Northwest Conference on Foreign Languages, at the University of Victoria (B.C.) in April, 1966.

NOTES: V

AFFIRMATION OF FORMLESSNESS

1 See, for example, Emil Merker, *Stifter* (Stuttgart, 1938), p. 69: "Ein Wunschtraum ist die Welt des Rosenhauses... im Sinne einer Steigerung, Verdichtung der Wirklichkeit dadurch, daß alles Gleichgültige, Zufällige, Unwesentliche daraus verbannt ist, *daß alles* bis zur Geringfügigkeit des letzten Gebrauchsgegenstandes durchgeformt, *Gestalt geworden ist*" (my italics).

2 Adalbert Stifter, *Der Nachsommer*, ed. Franz Hüller and others, in *Sämmtliche Werke*, VI, VII, VIII[1] (Prag und Reichenberg, 1901 ff.).

3 Cf. Erik Lunding, *Adalbert Stifter. Mit einem Anhang über Kierkegaard und die existentielle Literaturwissenschaft*. Studien zur Kunst und Existenz, no. 1 (Kjøbenhavn, 1946), p. 79: "[Es handelt] sich nicht um ein äußerlich schönheitliches, sondern um ein schönheitlich-sittliches Ideal. Das klassische Shaftesbury-Winckelmannsche Ideal der Kalokagathia beherrscht das Werk."

4 For a discussion of this episode, see Chapter III, pp. 38—45.
5 "Joseph, the Musician in Stifter's *Nachsommer*," *Monatshefte*, L (1958), 8.
6 *The Figure of the Musician in German Literature*. University of North Carolina Studies in the Germanic Languages and Literatures, no. 19 (Chapel Hill, 1956), p. 73. For biographical data on this subject, see Franz Schaffranke, "Adalbert Stifters Verhältnis zur Tonkunst," ASILO, IX (1960), 49—54.
7 Urban Roedl, *Adalbert Stifter* (Bern, 1958), pp. 351 f.: "der zitherspielende Jäger, der stellvertretend für alles Außergesellschaftliche am Rande der Nachsommerwelt sein liebenswürdiges Wesen treibt, ist ein Verwandter des Zigeunermädchens im Katzensilber und verkörpert wie sie *eine sehr geheime dichterische Sehnsucht*" (my italics).
8 This is in contrast to Mr. Tucker's unsubstantiated statement: "But in playing the zither, Joseph simultaneously *gives a form to music*" (p. 6; my italics). In the subsequent paragraph, Mr. Tucker wavers in his view and adds to our confusion by pointing out that music approaches nonexistence, or that it might be *tempus* itself, or that it should be defined as *Lautwerden*. While one readily agrees that music is based on "sound-production" (*Laut-werden*), the concept of music as both sounded and nonexistent seems philosophically abstruse. One may also object, it seems to me, to the notion that merely "in playing" Joseph gives a form to music; production of sound cannot be equated with production of form.
9 Reprinted by permission of the editors from *Modern Language Quarterly*, XXIX (Dec., 1968), 407—414.

NOTES: VI

THE MONSTROUS PAINTING

1 Adalbert Stifter, *Der Nachsommer*, ed. Franz Hüller and others, in *Sämmtliche Werke*, VI, VII, VIII¹ (Prag und Reichenberg, 1901 ff.).
2 In this novel about a young man who sets out to investigate all the formations of the earth, the sea, curiously, receives almost no attention. Though Stifter gives recognition to the sea as "vielleicht das Großartigste, was die Erde besitzt" (VIII, 208), he otherwise passes over it in silence, another sign of his reluctance to deal with something vast and equivocal and formless.

3 Erik Lunding, *Adalbert Stifter. Mit einem Anhang über Kierkegaard und die existentielle Literaturwissenschaft.* Studien zur Kunst und Existenz, no. 1 (Kjøbenhavn ,1946), p. 83: "Mit größter Sorgfalt hütet er sich davor, auch nur von ferne den Rand des Seins mit den Bedrohungen und Rätseln der Leere ahnen zu lassen."
4 Reprinted by permission of the editors from *Journal of English and Germanic Philology,* LXVIII (Jan., 1969), 92—99.

NOTES: VII

THE EQUIVOCAL LIGHT OF
THE *MARMORSAAL*

1 Adalbert Stifter, *Der Nachsommer,* ed. Franz Hüller and others, in *Sämmtliche Werke,* VI, VII, VIII¹ (Prag und Reichenberg, 1901 ff.).
2 Characteristic of early criticism of *Der Nachsommer* is the following excerpt taken from Heinrich Kurz, in the section "Adalbert Stifter" of his *Geschichte der neuesten deutschen Literatur,* vol. IV (Leipzig, 1873), pp. 784—88, quoted from Moriz Enzinger, *Adalbert Stifter im Urteil seiner Zeit* (Wien, 1968), p. 351: "[Der Nachsommer] verliert sich... gar zu sehr in die kleinlichste Detailmalerei, wobei er sogar Ähnliches, ja sogar das Nämliche häufig wiederholt und überhaupt *in eine endlose Breite verfällt*" (my italics).
3 For a discussion of this symbolism see Chapter III, pp. 47—49.
4 Toward the end of the novel a marriage feast is held in the *Marmorsaal,* which on this occasion takes on a secular aspect. This use of the hall may be regarded as an example of what Michael Johannes Böhler has termed a "Regressus ad profanum...die Bewegung vom Himmel zur Erde, vom überirdischen Absoluten zum irdisch Beschränkten" (*Formen und Wandlungen des Schönen. Untersuchungen zum Schönheitsbegriff Adalbert Stifters* [Bern, 1967], p. 7). During the celebration the floor is covered with green cloth, so no one need remove his shoes. Symbolically, the green cover temporarily suspends the sacredness of the hall, for green is the color of the living vegetation covering the earth, and suggests natural earthly reality. To be noted also is the rare moment of gentle humor when Risach parodies the earlier solemn statement of Heinrich ("Zu dem Ernste der Wolkenwände gesellt sich der Ernst der Wände

von Marmor") by proclaiming: "der Ernst des Marmors... dürfe nur in den Ernst des edelsten Weines nieder blicken" (VIII, 219).

5 W. H. Rey, "Das kosmische Erschrecken in Stifters Frühwerk," *Die Sammlung. Zeitschrift für Kultur und Erziehung*, VIII (Göttingen, 1953), 6—13, examines the "Kondor" to give evidence of Stifter's own fright at the vastness of the cosmos, a terror which was conquered through religious faith, as Rey illustrates by a brilliant analysis of Stifter's description of the eclipse of the sun on 8 July 1842. What Rey says about Stifter's spiritual conquest can also be applied to Heinrich at maturity: "Für den Dichter ist der Himmel, der ihn überwältigt, nicht leer. Für ihn ist das Furchtbare ein Attribut des Heiligen. In dem Schauer des Herzens vor der unheimlichen Entfremdung der Welt erlebt er nicht den Triumph des Nichts, sondern die Offenbarung Gottes" (p. 12).

6 So also Karl Josef Hahn, *Adalbert Stifter: Religiöses Bewußtsein und dichterisches Werk* (Halle, 1938), p. 27: "Nach seinem Denken kann Gott als Unendliches niemals angeschaut werden, die *unio mystica* ist seinem Wesen völlig entgegengesetzt.... Das Göttliche verehrt er nicht in seiner Transzendenz, sondern in der sichtbaren Auswirkung auf die gesamte Welt." By contrast, Hermann Augustin, *Adalbert Stifter und das christliche Weltbild*, (Basel, 1959), sees a strong element of mysticism pervading Stifter's entire work. Augustin's presentation is purely associative and too subjectively emotional to be useful to further scholarly attempts at exploring this theme.

7 Kurt Michel, *Adalbert Stifter und die transzendente Welt*, Schriftenreihe des ASILO, no. 9 (Graz-Wien, 1957), p. 104: "Mystik und Mysterium im vollen Sinn der christlichen Offenbarung sind Stifter fremd.... Mystik will personale unmittelbare Vereinigung mit Gott. Stifters Liebe aber gilt der Welt und ihren Dingen und damit erst mittelbar durch sie hindurch Gott."

8 Michel, p. 145: "Hier wird es offenbar, daß die übernatürliche Gnadenwelt, die ihren Höhepunkt in der *visio beatifica* hat, von ihm nicht existentiell erfaßt war."

9 Böhler, *Formen und Wandlungen des Schönen*, p. 95.

10 Böhler, p. 43.

11 More than any other image of formlessness, such as Joseph's music or Roland's painting (see Chapters V and VI above), the *Marmorsaal*, as the primary image of *Gestaltlosigkeit*, exerts the fascination of the numinous.

12 Reprinted by permission of the editors from *Journal of English and Germanic Philology*, LXIX (Jan., 1970), 108—117.

NOTES: VIII

THE HUMAN *GESTALTEN* AND THE FOOLS

1 Wolfgang Paulsen, "Adalbert Stifter und der *Nachsommer*," *Corona* (Durham, 1941), p. 250.
2 Horst Glaser, *Die Restauration des Schönen*, Germanistische Abhandlungen, no. 6 (Stuttgart, 1965), p. 60.
3 Glaser, p. 65: "Die Utopie erhält sich durch Schweigen schwebend über geschichtlichem Unrecht. Sie berichtet weiterhin *nur von Reichen*, so daß schließlich Armut und Unrecht in ihr vergessen sind." (Italics mine). To Glaser the novel is a lie in its pretensions at reconciliation between nature and man, and between person and person, class and class. See Glaser, pp. 63 f.: "Versöhnung zerfällt in die süßliche Lüge fröhlichen Beisammenseins und freudig getaner Arbeit." The denunciation of the "false" harmony depicted in this novel by the "reactionary" author is more an expression of the politically oriented critic's socialistic proclivities, than it is a literary criticism of objective validity. Other critics have evaluated the same phenomenon in a more positive way, as literature. See for example Walther Killy, *Wirklichkeit und Kunstcharakter* (München, 1963), p. 83: "Selten ist ein Buch so sehr und absichtsvoll gegen den Strich der Zeit geschrieben worden," and p. 84: "Er [Stifter] setzte dem Jahrhundert, an dem er litt wie alle Dichter, die schönste Utopie entgegen, die die deutsche Dichtung kennt." For an excellent review of Glaser's book, see Friedbert Aspetsberger, ASILO, XV (1966), 132—35.
4 Killy, p. 84. For a thorough exploration of Stifter's image of the ideal man see Joachim Müller, *Adalbert Stifter. Weltbild und Dichtung. Menschwerdung des Menschen* (Halle [Saale], 1956).
5 Hermann Kunisch, *Adalbert Stifter: Mensch und Wirklichkeit* (Berlin, 1950), p. 94. (Italics mine).
6 Müller, p. 19.
7 Michael Johannes Böhler, *Formen und Wandlungen des Schönen* (Bern, 1967), p. 43.
8 Killy, pp. 100 f.
9 Eric Blackall, *Adalbert Stifter: A Critical Study* (Cambridge, Eng., 1948), p. 330.
10 Dorothea Sieber, *Stifters "Nachsommer"* (Jena, 1927), p. 41.
11 See Hilde Cohn, "Symbole in Adalbert Stifters 'Studien' und 'Bunten Steinen,'" *Monatshefte*, XXXIII (1941), 245: "Die auffallende Wiederholung typischer Figuren an Stelle eines bunten Gestaltenreichtums be-

weist ja eben den symbolischen Charakter seiner Dichtung im Ganzen wie im Einzelnen."
12 Paul Hankamer, "Die Menschenwelt in Stifters Werk," DVLG, XVI (1938), 120.
13 Killy, p. 98.
14 Hankamer, p. 111.
15 Adalbert Stifter, *Der Nachsommer*, ed. Franz Hüller and others, in *Sämmtliche Werke*, VI, VII, VIII¹ (Prag und Reichenberg, 1901 ff.).
16 Sieber, pp. 55 f.
17 For a study of Stifter's use of the giving or withholding of names as a stylistic device see Marlene J. Norst, "Sinn und Bedeutung der Namengebung bei Adalbert Stifter," ASILO, XVI (1967), 90: "Es ist...die Namengebung als Stilmittel verwendet, worauf Stifter Wert legt. Das Aussprechen und Nichtaussprechen von Eigennamen ist ein Wesenszug der Welt, die in seinen Werken zum Ausdruck kommt."
18 Marianne Thalmann, "Das Menschentum in Stifters 'Haidedorf'." MLN, LXI (1946), 368.
19 Karlheinz Rossbacher, "Erzählstandpunkt und Personendarstellung bei Adalbert Stifter," ASILO, XVII (1968), 49 f.
20 See the explanation Heinrich gives for the fact that Mathilde and Natalie never wear earrings: "Wenn aber der Körper verwundet wird, um Schmuck in die Verletzung zu hängen, werde er Diener des Schmuckes" (VIII, 223).
21 "Aber es gibt auch ein Einerlei, welches so erhaben ist, daß es als Fülle die ganze Seele ergreift und als Einfachheit das All umschließt" (VII, 243).
22 Marianne Ludwig, *Stifter als Realist* (Basel, 1948), p. 7.
23 See Chapter VI, pp. 51 f.
24 Blackall, p. 330.
25 Otto Stoessl, *Adalbert Stifter: Eine Studie* (Stuttgart, 1925), p. 53: "niemand kann dieser weltlichen Heiligkeit Ehrfurcht und Glauben versagen."
26 Joseph Michels, *Adalbert Stifter: Leben, Werk und Wirken* (Berlin, 1939), p. 228.
27 Reprinted by permission of the editors from *Journal of English and Germanic Philology*, LXX (Jan., 1971), 86—101.

NOTES: IX. CONCLUSION

HEINRICH'S PROGRESS TOWARD THE *MARMORGESTALT*

[1] Erik Lunding, *Adalbert Stifter. Mit einem Anhang über Kierkegaard und die existentielle Literaturwissenschaft*. Studien zur Kunst und Existenz, no. 1 (Kjøbenhavn, 1946), pp. 79 f..

[2] Adalbert Stifter, *Der Nachsommer*, ed. Franz Hüller and others, in *Sämmtliche Werke*, VI, VII, VIII[1] (Prag und Reichenberg, 1901 ff.).

[3] Herbert Seidler, "Gestaltung und Sinn des Raumes in Stifters *Nachsommer*," *Studien und Interpretationen*, ed. Lothar Stiehm (Heidelberg, 1968), p. 218.

[4] Wilhelm Dehn, *Ding und Vernunft* (Bonn, 1969), p. 19.

[5] Carl Helbling, *Adalbert Stifter: Aufsätze* (St. Gallen, 1943), p. 81.

[6] Wilhelm Dehn, *Ding und Vernunft*, p. 20.

[7] "Ritualism and Motivic Development in Adalbert Stifter's *Nachsommer*," *Neophilologus*, XLVIII (1964), 314 f..

[8] Wolfgang Paulsen, "Adalbert Stifter und der *Nachsommer*," in *Corona* (Durham, 1941), p. 234.

SELECTED BIBLIOGRAPHY

This bibliography lists items which I consider to be milestones in the history of Stifter-scholarship, critical studies of particular relevance to *Der Nachsommer*, and recent works of general interest and importance.

Abbreviations:

ASILO   Adalbert Stifter-Institut des Landes Oberösterreich, Linz (publishes *Vierteljahrsschrift* and Schriftenreihe)
DVLG   *Deutsche Vierteljahrsschrift für Literaturwissenschaft und Geistesgeschichte*
GRM   *Germanisch-romanische Monatsschrift*
JEGP   *Journal of English and Germanic Philology*
MLN   *Modern Language Notes*
PMLA   *Publications of the Modern Language Association of America*

Edition:

Adalbert Stifter, *Der Nachsommer*, in *Sämmtliche Werke*, VI, VII, VIII[1] ed. Kamill Eben and Franz Hüller. Bibliothek Deutscher Schriftsteller aus Böhmen, ed. August Sauer *et al.* (Prag: J. G. Calve, 1901 ff.).

Literature on Stifter:

APRENT, JOHANNES. *Adalbert Stifter: Eine biographische Skizze*. 2nd. ed., ed. Moriz Enzinger. Nürnberg, 1955 [1st ed. Pest, 1869].
ARNOLD, LUDWIG. *Stifters "Nachsommer" als Bildungsroman, im Vergleich mit "Wilhelm Meister" und dem "Grünen Heinrich."* Gießener Beiträge zur Philologie, no. 65, Gießen, 1938.
ASPETSBERGER, FRIEDBERT. "Stifters Tautologien," ASILO, XV (1966), 23—44.
AUGUSTIN, HERMANN. *Adalbert Stifter und das christliche Weltbild*. Basel, 1959.

AUGUSTIN, HERMANN. *Dante, Goethe, Stifter. Das fromme Weltbild des Dichters.* Basel, 1944.
—. *Goethes und Stifters Nausikäa-Tragödie. Über die Urphänomene.* Basel, 1941.
BAHR, HERMANN. *Adalbert Stifter: Eine Entdeckung.* Zürich, 1919.
BERTRAM, ERNST. *Studien zu Adalbert Stifters Novellentechnik.* 2nd. ed. Dortmund, 1966 [1st ed. 1907].
BIETAK, WILHELM. "Probleme der Biedermeier-Dichtung," *Neue Beiträge zum Grillparzer- und Stifter-Bild* (Graz-Wien, 1965), pp. 5—20.
BLACKALL, ERIC ALBERT. *Adalbert Stifter: A Critical Study.* Cambridge, England, 1948.
BÖHLER, MICHAEL JOHANNES. *Formen und Wandlungen des Schönen: Untersuchungen zum Schönheitsbegriff Adalbert Stifters.* Europäische Hochschulschriften, Reihe 1: Deutsche Literatur und Germanistik, no. 6. Bern, 1967.
—. "Die Individualität in Stifters Spätwerk: Ein ästhetisches Problem," DVLG, XLIII (1969), 652—684.
BOLLNOW, OTTO FRIEDRICH. "Der *Nachsommer* und der Bildungsgedanke des Biedermeier," in *Beiträge zur Bildung und Sprache im geistigen Sinn. Festschrift zum 80. Geburtstag von Ernst Otto.* Berlin, 1957, pp. 14—33.
BRAUN, FELIX. "Reflections on Stifter's *Nachsommer*," *German Life and Letters,* IV (1939), 25—32.
CASTLE, EDUARD. "Motivvariationen in Stifters Erzählkunst," *Adalbert-Stifter-Almanach für 1947* (Wien, 1947), pp. 35—57.
COHN, HILDE. "Symbole in Adalbert Stifters 'Studien' und 'Bunten Steinen,'" *Monatshefte,* XXXIII (1941), 241—264.
CYSARZ, HERBERT. "Der Dichter des seienden Seins: Adalbert Stifter," *Welträtsel im Wort. Studien zur europäischen Dichtung und Philosophie.* Wien, 1948, pp. 246—276.
DEHN, WILHELM. *Ding und Vernunft: Zur Interpretation von Stifters Dichtung.* Literatur und Wirklichkeit, vol. III. Bonn, 1969.
EISENMEIER, EDUARD. *Adalbert Stifter Bibliographie.* Schriftenreihe des ASILO, no. 21. Linz, 1964.
ENZINGER, MORIZ. *Adalbert Stifter im Urteil seiner Zeit. Festgabe zum 28. Jänner, 1968.* Sitzungsberichte der österreichischen Akademie der Wissenschaften, Philosophisch-Historische Klasse, vol. 256. Graz, Wien, Köln, 1968.
—. *Gesammelte Aufsätze zu Adalbert Stifter.* Wien, 1967.
FEHLAU, ULAND EVERETT. "Symbolism in Adalbert Stifter's Works," JEGP, XXXIX (1940), 239—255.
FISCHER, KURT GERHARD. *Adalbert Stifter: Die Pädagogik des Menschenmöglichen.* Schriftenreihe des ASILO, no. 17. Linz, 1962.

FISCHER, KURT GERHARD. *Adalbert Stifter: Psychologische Beiträge zur Biographie.* Schriftenreihe des ASILO, no. 16. Linz, 1961.

—. *Adalbert Stifters Leben und Werk in Briefen und Dokumenten.* Frankfurt, 1962.

—. "Bildungsprobleme, dem *Nachsommer* nachgesagt," ASILO, VIII (1959), 45—49.

FRODL, HERMANN. "Adalbert Stifter und das barocke Erbe," ASILO, XV (1966), 98—116.

—. "Adalbert Stifters Shakespeare-Erlebnis," ASILO, XVII (1968), 241—254.

FUERST, NORBERT. "Three German Novels of Education. II: Stifter's *Nachsommer*," *Monatshefte*, XXXVIII (1946), 413—425.

GILLESPIE, GERALD. "Ritualism and Motivic Development in Adalbert Stifter's *Nachsommer*," *Neophilologus*, XLVIII (1964), 312—322.

GLASER, HORST ALBERT. *Die Restauration des Schönen: Stifters "Nachsommer."* Germanistische Abhandlungen, no. 6. Stuttgart, 1965.

GRÖBLE, SUSI. *Schuld und Sühne im Werk Adalbert Stifters.* Basler Studien zur deutschen Sprache und Literatur, no. 28. Bern, 1965.

GROLMAN, ADOLF VON. *Adalbert Stifters Romane.* DVLG, Buchreihe, vol. 7. Halle (Saale), 1926.

GROSSCHOPF, ALOIS. *Adalbert Stifter: Leben, Werk, Landschaft.* Linz, 1967.

GUMP, MARGARETE. *Stifters Kunstanschauung.* Berlin, 1927.

GUNDOLF, FRIEDRICH. *Adalbert Stifter.* Halle (Saale), 1931.

HAHN, KARL JOSEF. *Adalbert Stifter: Religiöses Bewußtsein und dichterisches Werk.* Halle (Saale), 1938.

HAHN, WALTHER. "Zu Stifters Konzept der Schönheit: Brigitta," ASILO, XIX (1970), 149—159.

HALLAMORE, G. JOYCE. "The Symbolism of the Marble Muse in Stifter's *Nachsommer*," PMLA, LXXIV (1959), 398—405.

HANKAMER, PAUL. "Die Menschenwelt in Stifters Werk," DVLG, XVI (1938), 95—125.

HEBBEL, FRIEDRICH. *Sämtliche Werke*, ed. R. M. Werner. Berlin, 1901 ff.

HEIN, ALOIS RAIMUND. *Adalbert Stifter: Sein Leben und seine Werke.* 2nd ed. Wien, 1952 [1st ed. Prag, 1904].

HELBLING, CARL. *Adalbert Stifter: Aufsätze.* St. Gallen, 1943.

HERMAND, JOST. *Die literarische Formenwelt des Biedermeier.* Gießen, 1958.

HERTLING, GUNTER. "Grenzübergang und Raumverletzung: Zur Zentralthematik in Adalbert Stifters 'Studien,'" ASILO, XVI (1967), 61—77.

HIMMEL, HELLMUTH. "Probleme der österreichischen Biedermeiernovellistik: Ein Beitrag zur Erkenntnis der historischen Stellung Adalbert Stifters," ASILO, XII (1963), 36—59.

HOFMANNSTHAL, HUGO VON. "Stifters *Nachsommer*," *Ariadne. Jahrbuch der Nietzsche-Gesellschaft* (München, 1925), pp. 27—35.

HOHOFF, CURT. *Adalbert Stifter: Seine dichterischen Mittel und die Prosa des neunzehnten Jahrhunderts.* Düsseldorf, 1949.

HÖLLERER, WALTER. "Adalbert Stifter," *Zwischen Klassik und Moderne. Lachen und Weinen in der Dichtung einer Übergangszeit.* Stuttgart, 1958, pp. 357—377.

HOLSKE, ALAN. "Stifter and the Biedermeier Crisis," *Studies in Honor of J. A. Walz.* Lancaster, Pa., 1941, pp. 256—90.

HÜLLER, FRANZ. "Einführung in Adalbert Stifter, *Der Nachsommer*," *Adalbert Stifter, Sämmtliche Werke*, vol. VI. Prag, 1921.

KILLY, WALTHER. "Utopische Gegenwart," *Wirklichkeit und Kunstcharakter: Neun Romane des neunzehnten Jahrhunderts.* München, 1963, pp. 83—103.

KLATT, FRITZ. "Stifter und das Dämonische," *Dichtung und Volkstum (Euphorion)*, XL (1939), 276—295.

KLÄUI, ELISABETH. *Gestaltung und Formen der Zeit im Werk Adalbert Stifters.* Bern, 1969.

KOHLSCHMIDT, WERNER. "Leben und Tod in Stifters Studien," *Form und Innerlichkeit: Beiträge zur Geschichte und Wirkung der deutschen Klassik und Romantik.* Bern, 1955, pp. 210—232 [first publ. in *Dichtung und Volkstum (Euphorion)*, XXXVI (1935)].

KORFF, FRIEDRICH WILHELM. *Diastole und Systole: Zum Thema Jean Paul und Adalbert Stifter.* Basler Studien zur deutschen Sprache und Literatur, no. 37. Bern, 1969.

KOSCH, WILHELM. *Adalbert Stifter und die Romantik.* 2nd ed. Nymwegen, 1946 [1st ed. Prag, 1905].

KRACKER-SCHWARZENFELDT, INGRID. "Das Gestaltungsprinzip in Stifters Werk," ASILO, IV (1955), 161—179.

KRÖKEL, FRITZ. "Die Magie des Schönen und das Erdenglück," ASILO, XXII (1963), 108—120.

KUNISCH, HERMANN. *Adalbert Stifter, Mensch und Wirklichkeit: Studien zu seinem klassischen Stil.* Berlin, 1950.

KÜPPER, PETER. "Literatur und Langeweile: Zur Lektüre Stifters," *Adalbert Stifter: Studien und Interpretationen: Gedenkschrift zum 100. Todestage*, ed. Lothar Stiehm. Heidelberg, 1968, pp. 171—188.

LANGE, VICTOR. "Stifter: *Der Nachsommer*," *Der deutsche Roman vom Barock bis zur Gegenwart: Struktur und Geschichte*, ed. Benno von Wiese. Düsseldorf, 1963, vol. II, pp. 34—75.

LUDWIG, MARIANNE. *Stifter als Realist: Untersuchung über die Gegenständlichkeit im "Beschriebenen Tännling."* Basler Studien zur deutschen Sprache und Literatur, no. 7. Basel, 1948.

LUNDING, ERIK PETER. *Adalbert Stifter. Mit einem Anhang über Kierkegaard und die existentielle Literaturwissenschaft.* Studien zur Kunst und Existenz, no. 1. Kjøbenhavn, 1946.

—. "Forschungsbericht: Probleme und Ergebnisse der Stifterforschung 1945—54," *Euphorion,* IL (1955), 203—244.

MARTINI, FRITZ. *Deutsche Literatur im bürgerlichen Realismus 1848—1898.* Epochen der deutschen Literatur. Geschichtliche Darstellungen, V/2. Stuttgart, 1962, 499—556.

MATZKE, FRANZ. *Die Landschaft in der Dichtung Adalbert Stifters.* Eger, 1932.

MERKER, EMIL. *Adalbert Stifter.* Stuttgart, 1938.

METTLER, HEINRICH. *Natur in Stifters frühen "Studien": Zu Stifters gegenständlichem Stil.* Zürcher Beiträge zur deutschen Literatur- und Geistesgeschichte, vol. 31. Zürich, 1968.

MEYER, HERMANN. *Der Typus des Sonderlings in der deutschen Literatur.* München, 1963, pp. 163—189 (1st ed. Amsterdam, 1943, pp. 121—142).

MICHEL, KURT. *Adalbert Stifter und die transzendente Welt: Ein Beitrag zur Erhellung der Existenz des Dichters.* Schriftenreihe des ASILO, no. 9. Graz-Wien, 1957.

MICHELS, JOSEF. *Adalbert Stifter: Leben, Werk und Wirken.* Wien-Berlin-Leipzig, 1939.

MÜHLHER, ROBERT. "Et in Arcadia Ego: Das Bild der Gartenlaube bei Adalbert Stifter," *Adalbert Stifter: Studien und Interpretationen: Gedenkschrift zum 100. Todestage,* ed. Lothar Stiehm. Heidelberg, 1968, pp. 189—202.

MÜLLER, GÜNTHER. "Stifter, der Dichter der Spätromantik," *Jahrbuch des Verbandes der Vereine katholischer Akademiker zur Pflege der katholischen Weltanschauung* (Augsburg, 1924), pp. 18—77.

MÜLLER, JOACHIM. *Adalbert Stifter: Weltbild und Dichtung.* Halle (Saale), 1956.

—. "Das Liebesgespräch in Adalbert Stifters Epik," *Wirkendes Wort,* VIII (1957/58), 20—30.

—. *Vergleichende Studien zur Menschenauffassung und Menschendarstellung Gottfried Kellers und Adalbert Sifters.* Weida (Thür.), 1930.

MUSCHG, WALTER. "Das Farbenspiel von Stifters Melancholie," *Studien zur tragischen Literaturgeschichte.* Bern, 1965, pp. 180—204 [1st ed. Bern, 1948].

NORST, MARLENE. "Sinn und Bedeutung der Namengebung bei Adalbert Stifter, dargestellt an Hand einer Untersuchung der Novelle 'Der Waldsteig,'" *ASILO,* XVI (1967), 90—99.

NOVOTNY, FRITZ. *Adalbert Stifter als Maler.* Wien, 1941.

PASCAL, ROY. "Adalbert Stifter: *Indian Summer*," *The German Novel*. Manchester, 1956, pp. 52—75.

PAULSEN, WOLFGANG. "Adalbert Stifter und der *Nachsommer*," *Corona*. *Festschrift für Samuel Singer*. Durham, N.C., 1941, pp. 228—251.

PETRY, URSULA. "Die Entstehung einer Landschaft: Zur Dialektik des Drinnen und Draußen bei Adalbert Stifter," ASILO, XVIII (1969), 117—138.

PREISENDANZ, WOLFGANG. "Die Erzählfunktion der Naturdarstellung bei Stifter," *Wirkendes Wort*, XVI (1966), 407—418.

PRIVAT, KARL. *Adalbert Stifter: Sein Leben in Selbstzeugnissen, Briefen und Berichten*. Berlin, 1946.

REHM, WALTHER. *Nachsommer: Zur Deutung von Stifters Dichtung*. Bern-München, 1951.

—. "Wirklichkeitsdemut und Dingmystik," *Logos*, XIX (1930), 297—358.

REQUADT, PAUL. *Das Sinnbild der Rosen in Stifters Dichtung: Zur Deutung seiner Farbensymbolik*. Abhandlungen der Akademie der Wissenschaften und der Literatur, Jg. 1952, no. 2. Wiesbaden, 1952, pp. 17—54.

REY, WILLY H. "Das kosmische Erschrecken in Stifters Frühwerk," *Die Sammlung. Zeitschrift für Kultur und Erziehung*, VIII (1953), 6—13.

ROEDL, URBAN. *Adalbert Stifter: Geschichte seines Lebens*. Bern, 1958 [1st ed. Berlin, 1936].

ROSSBACHER, KARLHEINZ. "Erzählstandpunkt und Personendarstellung bei Adalbert Stifter," ASILO, XVII (1968), 47—58.

RYCHNER, MAX. "Stifters 'Nachsommer,'" *Interpretationen III: Deutsche Romane von Grimmelshausen bis Musil*, ed. Jost Schillemeit. Frankfurt a. M., 1966, pp. 190—202 [first published in *Neue Schweizer Rundschau*, NF. 16 (1948/49), 32—45; reprinted in Rychner, *Welt im Wort*. Zürich, 1949, pp. 157—180].

SCHAFFRANKE, FRANZ. "Adalbert Stifters Verhältnis zur Tonkunst," ASILO, IX (1960), 49—54.

SCHMIDT, ARNO. "Der sanfte Unmensch," *Dya na Sore: Gespräche in einer Bibliothek*. Karlsruhe, 1958, pp. 194—229.

SCHÖNDORFER, ULRICH. "Stifters Synthese humanistischer und realistischer Bildung," ASILO, XVII (1968) 13—18.

SCHOOLFIELD, GEORGE. *The Figure of the Musician in German Literature*. University of North Carolina Studies in the Germanic Languages and Literatures, no. 19. Chapel Hill, 1956.

SEEBASS, FRIEDRICH. "Über Stifters Dichtung," *Deutsche Rundschau*, LXXVIII (Oct. 1952), 1079.

SEIDLER, HERBERT. "Die Bedeutung der Mitte in Stifters *Nachsommer*," ASILO, VI (1957), 59—86.

—. "Die Enthüllung des Dichterischen," ASILO, XVII (1968), 7—11.

—. "Die Natur in der Dichtung Stifters," ASILO, XVII (1968), 223—240.

SEIDLER, HERBERT. "Gestaltung und Sinn des Raumes in Stifters *Nachsommer*," *Adalbert Stifter: Studien und Interpretationen. Gedenkschrift zum 100. Todestage*, ed. Lothar Stiehm. Heidelberg, 1968, pp. 203—226.

—. "Wandlungen des deutschen Bildungsromans im neunzehnten Jahrhundert," *Wirkendes Wort*, XI (1961), 148—162.

SIEBER, DOROTHEA. *Stifters "Nachsommer."* Jenaer Germanistische Forschungen, no. 10. Jena, 1927.

SPALDING, KEITH. "Adalbert Stifter," *German Men of Letters*, V, ed. Alex Natan. London, 1969, 183—206.

STAIGER, EMIL. "Reiz und Maß: Das Beispiel Stifters," *Adalbert Stifter: Studien und Interpretationen: Gedenkschrift zum 100. Todestage*, ed. Lothar Stiehm. Heidelberg, 1968, pp. 7—22.

—. *Adalbert Stifter*. "Der Nachsommer," *Meisterwerke deutscher Sprache aus dem neunzehnten Jahrhundert*. Zürich, 1961, pp. 186—201 [1st ed. 1943].

STEFFEN, KONRAD. *Adalbert Stifter: Deutungen*. Basel, 1955.

STEFL, MAX. "Adalbert Stifters Gestalten," *Homo homini homo. Festschrift für Joseph E. Drexel*, ed. W. R. Beyer. München, 1966, pp. 25—30.

STERN, JOSEPH PETER. "Adalbert Stifters ontologischer Stil," *Adalbert Stifter: Studien und Interpretationen: Gedenkschrift zum 100. Todestage*, ed. Lothar Stiehm. Heidelberg, 1968, pp. 103—120.

—. "Propitiations: Adalbert Stifter," *Re-Interpretations: Seven Studies in Nineteenth Century German Literature*. London, 1964, pp. 239—300.

STOWELL, JOHN D. "Some Archetypes in Stifter's *Der Nachsommer*: An Attempt at Restoring Fictional Interest," *Seminar*, VI (March, 1970), 31—47.

STRAUMANN-WINDLER, HEDWIG. *Stifters Narren: Zum Problem der Spätromantik*. Zürich, 1952.

STRICH, FRITZ. "Adalbert Stifter und unsere Zeit," *Der Dichter und die Zeit*. Bern, 1947, pp. 291—326.

TEUTSCHMANN, HEINRICH. *Adalbert Stifters gegenwärtiges Wort*. Goetheanum Bücherei. Dornach (Schweiz), 1967.

THALMANN, MARIANNE. "Adalbert Stifters Raumerlebnis," *Monatshefte*, XXXVIII (1946), 103—111.

—. "Das Menschentum in Stifters Haidedorf," *MLN*, LXI (1946), 361—372.

THOMAS, WERNER. "Stifters Landschaftskunst in Sprache und Malerei," *Der Deutschunterricht*, VIII/3 (1956), 12—27.

TUCKER, HARRY, JR. "Joseph, the Musician in Stifter's *Nachsommer*," *Monatshefte*, L (1958), 1—8.

VANCSA, KURT. "Stifter im Zwielicht: Ein Forschungsbericht," ASILO, VII (1958), 92—105.

VANCSA, KURT. "Ist Stifters dichterische Welt eine Utopie?" ASILO, V (1956), 153—162.

VORBACH, BERTA. *Adalbert Stifter und die Frau.* Reichenberg, 1936.

WEYDT, GÜNTHER. "Ist der *Nachsommer* ein geheimer Ofterdingen?" GRM, VIII, (1958), 72—81.

WINTERSTEIN, ALFRED. *Adalbert Stifter: Persönlichkeit und Werk: Eine tiefenpsychologische Studie.* Wien, 1946.

WOLBRANDT, CHRISTINE. *Der Raum in der Dichtung Adalbert Stifters.* Zürcher Beiträge zur deutschen Literatur- und Geistesgeschichte, no. 29. Zürich, 1967.

ZOLDESTER, PHILIP H. *Adalbert Stifters Weltanschauung.* Europäische Hochschulschriften. Reihe 1: Deutsche Literatur und Germanistik, no. 19. Bern, 1970.

www.ingramcontent.com/pod-product-compliance
Lightning Source LLC
Chambersburg PA
CBHW031317150426
43191CB00005B/265